A GIFT TO SHARE

Simple Truths Every Human Should Know

Claudia Denise Scott

Order this book online at www.trafford.com
or email orders@trafford.com

Most Trafford titles are also available at major online book retailers.

Printed in the United States of America.

ISBN: 978-1-4269-5818-2 (sc)
ISBN: 978-1-4269-5819-9 (hc)
ISBN: 978-1-4269-5820-5 (e)

Library of Congress Control Number: 2011903454

Trafford rev. 03/03/2011

Trafford PUBLISHING® **www.trafford.com**

North America & international
toll-free: 1 888 232 4444 (USA & Canada)
phone: 250 383 6864 • fax: 812 355 4082

CONTENTS

LOVE LETTERS FROM GOD

DEDICATION

I would like to dedicate my book to JESUS who kept me safe and gave me this wonderful gift to share and in loving memory of my grandfather, whom I was named after. It took his death to know that I had had a stroke. He is dearly missed but we will meet again on that glorious day.

Claude Marion Hobbs Sr.

I would also like to thank, Frank Boockholdt for giving me the courage to begin my quest for being God's soldier and helping me seek God's plan for my future. And last but not least I'd like to thank my wonderful husband, Jeffery W. Scott, who has been by my side through it all and I love very much!

INTRODUCTION

If you're tired of being sick or just sick and tired; within these pages are the truths you must learn. God says, "My people perish for lack of knowledge", Are you perishing? The truth shall set you free! Accepting Christ Jesus as Lord and Savior is a beginning not an end!

I wish to share this with everyone for a very special reason... it is my heart felt desire to have you know how much God cares for you and his overwhelming generosity to you through his son Jesus Christ. It's Christ's arms that reach out to you today, to hold you and embrace you in His incredible Love. Jesus is God's gift to humanity and it is through Him alone that each of us can experience the joy of being forgiven. Jesus bore our sickness, carried our diseases and forgave our sins. Our deliverance for soul and body comes from Christ that died on the cross that we might be saved and healed. It was not the nails that held him to the cross, it was his love for us. Each and every one of us. For it is not his wish that no one should perish. It is my prayer that this joy will be yours.

Thank you for allowing me to share some of the wisdom God has given me. I hope you will use this book as an instruction manual for your Instruction Book---The BIBLE...

Basic Instructions Before Leaving Earth. The main question is do you believe the Bible is God's Word. For the things I will share with you is not my opinion, but God's Word. If you believe in the Bible you must believe in all the bible, for it is not a buffet to pick and choose what you like and don't like. Remember Jesus is the same yesterday, today and forever. Now before I begin I'd like to tell you Satan has tried several times to kill me, I plead the blood in Jesus name so he couldn't. Next, he tried to use God's Word against me but God showed me I'm to share this and not to keep my mouth shut so that's what I'm going to do now. God lead me to read Acts 2:17-18; In the last days, God says, I will pour out my Spirit on all people.

Your sons and daughters will prophesy, your young men will dream dreams. Even on my servants, both men and women, I will pour out my Spirit in those days, and they will prophesy. Please begin with an open mind then ask for wisdom, knowledge and understanding also pray to rebuke and bind all evil from the hindrence of God's will for you and loosen God's will, word, purpose and spirit for your life in Jesus Name. Do you have your Bible? Dust it off and buckle up for a roller coaster ride through scripture. You need to realize you came with an instruction manual. You will find all the answers to life there. Learn how to use it, learn how to access your special features! Like other things if you don't read the instructions you can only use the basic features.

We've been trotting down life's road with relaxed reins. It's time to jerk the slack out of our reins and take control. It's time to get down to God's business. It's time we claim kingdom force. Before I'm through sharing the truth you'll know how to do this and be a good soldier for Jesus Christ. We're in a spiritual war, if you do not train you will continue to be defeated. God gives us all we need to know if we'll just seek to find. We have lost loved ones, friends, and even blinded Christians wondering in this dark world in danger of being eaten by the wolf waiting in ambush. We need to learn God's Word on his promises and protection. Remember, God tells us my people perish for lack of knowledge. Just like man's law tells us ignorance of the law doesn't make you not guilty, God's word is the same. So, I would like to share the knowledge the Lord shared with me. Without this knowledge we're walking blindly to the dangers of this dark and evil world. Getting blindsided on life's intersections, not seeing that satan has set them up. I'm a friend of man and God. This is an urgent message that we must share with everyone. We need all God's friends and followers help!! May God bless you and give you strength.

Everyone wonders why this or why that? No one seems to have any answers. Why are our children so rebellious? You may hear someone say, "Well in my day children did not act this way". Well, in our day society has created our children's actions. There has been no answers to the questions man seeks, because we are looking in the wrong places for the answers. Who am I?, Where did I come from? And why am I here? Do you actually believe we have no purpose? Do you believe we just exist? Basic truths are revealed not thought out in any human mind!! They come from God, not man! The whole world has been deceived! But God has told us this since the beginning. For this war is not flesh and blood. Don't take my word for it. Research it for yourself. But beware anyone involved in knowing the truth will be a target for the central character!! Please pass this knowledge on to everyone, the message is now----the message is urgent!!! Anyone who has dominated history as he has can not be ignored, especially in these last days. Consider what is said about this clever character SATAN!! To do so maybe the peril of our very lives.

May God bless America and forgive her for she knows not what she does. The seeds of weakening have been sown and are taking root. The more sinful a culture becomes the less endurance it has. Results, if not changed---removal of God's blessing!!! Now, American's wonder why terrorism is hitting home and why the American dream is fleeting. What about home of the free and land of the brave or in God we trust? We need God's grace. Have we totally forgotten what this once great country is based on? Our founding father's wanted man's government out of God's business not God out of our business!! The USA no longer practices it's motto: "IN GOD WE TRUST". We have tolerated and even defended the subtle forces of evil in our land. God's word tells us if my people will humble themselves and repent of their evil ways I will hear them and heal their land. WAKE UP AMERICA BEFORE IT'S TOO LATE!!!

SUMMARY

Before we begin our Roller coaster ride; I want to share my brief summary of what my book is about and my personal testimony for Jesus Christ. First, I began with a short version of my life and how I received the knowledge and wisdom that I would like to share. I want the readers to know it was revealed and not taught to me by any man. The rest of the book is a quick roller coaster ride through scripture. Sort of an instruction manual on how to use the information in the Bible. Humans are always seeking answers to age-old questions. These answers are so simple but people go lifetimes without ever finding the truth. They are always seeking but never finding. Always looking for love in the wrong places. Always looking for that missing something that they can't put their finger on. Trying to fill a void with materials things and unfulfilling relationships. Humans are always buying self-help books, but never learn the simple truth. Taking man's opinion over God's word. It's time to get with the program. God's plan for humans is simple. Let's take a look at an example:

THE LORD'S PRAYER

OUR FATHER WHICH ART IN HEAVEN(Tells us who to pray to)---HALLOWED BE THY NAME (Tells us to praise the father)---THY KINGDOM COME THY WILL BE DONE ON EARTH AS IS IN HEAVEN (This passage tells us our life here as God's children should be as it is in heaven. How is heaven? No worry, no sickness, no pain, no poor, no wanting. Our Heavenly Father provides our needs if we obey his commands. JESUS gives us the power for this on earth as it is in heaven. III John 2--Beloved I wish above all things that thou prospereth and be in health even as thou soul prosperth. If we as humans would only accept our fathers inheritance for us. Like human fathers his hands are tied for his children if they don't come to him and accept his gifts.)---GIVE US THIS DAY

OUR DAILY BREAD(He wants to provide for us if we'll only allow him to.)---
FORGIVE OUR TRESPASSES AS WE FORGIVE THEM THAT TRESPASS AGAINST US(We must learn to forgive to be forgiven. Unforgiveness is one of the causes of hindered prayers.)---LEAD US NOT INTO TEMPTATION BUT DELIVER US FROM EVIL (Learn God's plan of protection. Learn who and what evil is. Learn how to fight. Like buying a security system, they don't work if you don't turn them on. It's always helpful to read your instructions.)---FOR THINE IS THE KINGDOM THE POWER AND THE GLORY (Give God the praise and glory.)---FOREVER AND EVER IN JESUS NAME AMEN---Jesus tells us to ask the father in his name. It also tells we have not because we ask not. God is seeking a relationship with his children. There's nothing he wouldn't do for a faithful child. Just as human fathers love their children, God loves us very much and will provide for us if we will only allow him to. Jesus tells just prove me. Let me show you the way. Let me guide you in truth. Just think if every human followed his instruction book it would be heaven here on earth! There would be no sin and guess what sin causes

death and destruction. Think of how this world is right now. Then think of how God's plan would have this world to be. It can be, if we will only follow the plan. People pay millions for help and the truth of grace is a cost free gift never opened by most humans. We're living in the last days, time is growing very short. Our father is so sad that his children are perishing for lack of knowledge. Parents can relate to this through their rebellious children. It hurts so much to see our children getting involved with the wrong crowd. We know it will lead to trouble but they seem to know it all and don't want parents telling them anything. This is the same way humans are treating our heavenly Father. He can't and won't force his children to be blessed or help them if they won't even talk to him. But they're quick to blame him when disaster hits, blame him for their own stupid choices. He has given all the answers to how and why but they don't read his love letters. They throw them to the side and sometimes when things get really bad they'll call home for help. See you have not because you ask not or you ask for selfish things that don't line up with the word of God. As a parent don't you want to talk to your children and be a part of their lives, well guess what God does too! Don't wait for bad times to call home, call just because you care. Call daily to say hello, I love you Lord. Thank you for everything.

Even people that are not a child of God wants to blame him for their problems. Being a good person won't qualify you as a child of God. Jesus died to bridge the gap that Adam caused for us to have a relationship with the Father once again. Without accepting Jesus as Lord and Savior we can only call out for him to save us. He only hears that from a sinner that has not accepted Jesus. After accepting Jesus then you become an adopted child of God and you have rights to all of the promises, learn them and how to use them all. Know that you are no longer of this dark world. Know that you belong to the kingdom of God and you are kingdom representatives here on earth. Now as a child of God we can have a relationship with the Father through the shed blood of Jesus Christ. We can talk to him anytime, anyplace and we should talk to him as we do a friend, for he is our best friend forever. Like Jesus, we are to do the Father's will in the name of Jesus.

You may ask for my qualifications to write this book. My knowledge was inspired by the Holy Spirit. A gift to share not to sit on a shelf. I would say my book is for personal growth, but different because it can be used as reference also. It contains a short story at the beginning and least to say unique in contents. If God be for us who can be against us. Also God's word tells me as child of God I'll be successful at everything I put my hands to.

MY PERSONAL TESTIMONY FOR JESUS CHRIST

II TIMOTHY 1:8

So do not be ashamed to testify about our Lord, or shamed of me his prisoner. But join with me in suffering for the gospel, by the power of God, who has saved us and called us to a Holy life not because of anything we have done but because of his own purpose and grace. This grace was given us in Christ Jesus before the beginning of time but it has now been revealed through the appearance of our Savior, Christ Jesus.

My name is Claudia Denise Scott. I was always close to Jesus; as far back as I can remember. I was saved by accepting Jesus as my personal Lord and Savior in March of 1977. I became pregnant and had twins in August of 1978, which made it very hard to

attend church alone with two babies. I finally gave up and started missing church. I always prayed and ask Jesus to take care of my family. The years past and I became farther from God. My brother was shot Dec. 4th, 1995. It should have been a fatal shot under his arm by a 306 rifle. It was called a hunting accident. He didn't even stay in the hospital over night, but he still carries the bullet in his back. Two years before this on Dec. 4th, 1993, he had a brush with death in a truck accident. His tire blew out; he lost control and rolled his small truck three times. Needless to say the truck was totaled . What should have been a fatal accident left him and two children just shaken and very thankful. I told him each time that God was always looking over us. He wanted to know if his dead grandmother could be his guardian angel. I wasn't sure of that answer at that time, so I started researching mythology. Now this search began in the spring of 1996. Once I began searching it seemed I had a mission to finish. I knew enough to say seek and ye shall find. I visited the local library. There the wheels of my mission began to turn. I found the book "SATAN ALIVE AND WELL ON PLANET EARTH" by Hal Lindsey. Boy, that was an eye opener. Before this, I thought of satan in the context of Hell and not in the realization of present tense. Everything started falling into place. I prayed for wisdom, understanding, and knowledge. My next stop was at the Amen Corner our local christian book store. I was led to a book "ANGELS AROUND US" by Douglas Connelly. This answered my brother's question. Now, my search that began with his question was not finished, because it had became much more. I had always had dreams during my life leading to do certain things. At that time, I was having problems with my daughter. She lived with her grandmother and she was allowing her to do things that I didn't approve of and I tried to handle it my way. It had gotten to the point where I wouldn't even speak to her or my parents. I began having dreams of things to do and things to write; now at this time my husband, Jeffery, was in a rock band called Talon. The first thing I wrote was a song for the band. It came to me in pieces. I kept a paper by my bed and wrote it down when I woke up. Then I put it all together. Next, I was led to buy my daughter the angel book for her 18th birthday. God gave me what to write to her in the front pages. But for some reason God told me I had to get it to her immediately. He urged me not wait for her birthday on Aug. 18th. Remember I wasn't speaking to my parents or her so when I took it to my mother's at 6a.m. one morning it was shocking to them. My heart was so troubled and heavy for some unknown reason. I gave it to her telling her through my tears to fight satan in Jesus name. I wouldn't leave until she promised to do it and for her to forgive me. I also asked my parents forgiveness, not knowing at the time, that this had to be done before God could give me my gift I was to receive. Little did I know satan was trying to win my daughter. Jesus put a stop to that, that very day! I began dreaming about a message I had to get out to everyone. I had not attended church in over 20 years, so what I received was God sent and a gift that I want to share with everyone who will listen. My message was of the last days. I woke from a dream to read Timothy's. The message was Jesus is coming soon!! II Timothy 3:1-5 tells of the last days. Since I hadn't been to church no one had told me preachers were saying this for at least the last 15 years. I wrote fliers about this and had copies made. My son was going to help me pass them out. The next night I woke from a dream to go back and reread II Timothy. My message was incomplete for I had missed something. Sure enough, at the end of II Timothy 4:21 I found my first name Claudia. In the bible, when God called people to do things for him he changed their names. Everyone had always known me by my middle name Denise. My first name Claudia was there at the end of the message of the last days. I claimed it in Jesus name. I began telling everyone about it. This was an awesome thought. I was told that the message was finished for this was the final part that would prove the message is real, is urgent and is NOW!!! I began to question, "This can't be real", "this can't mean me", surely, this is a coincidence", "why me?". I was led to look up, in the bible dictionary, the other names with mine in II Timothy. All the names except mine had a place and date on them. Claudia was a Christian woman saluting Timotheus. WOW! That's what my message was about Timothy's the last days. JESUS RETURN IS NOW!! This was a little hard to swallow. I was thinking can this be real. And then I was led to read II Timothy 1:8. After that I never questioned it again. I didn't sleep for days and I wasn't tired. I was led to buy a new bible. I read the whole new testament in three days and underlined parts. Then I put the underlined parts together and they read like a book. I began doing things I couldn't remember doing. I never stopped talking about God and the last days. I saw things other people couldn't see. There's a spiritual war going on around us daily. I was allowed to see some of it. I was being prepared for a battle that I didn't know was coming. My husband played drums in the band. They were looking for a bass player and one was coming for an audition. My husband had made the statement that he would do anything to have one great record and be famous. I warned him to be careful of what he says for you may get what you ask for. The day that bass player walked in my front door, it was like satan himself was there. No one else picked up on the things he said and done but me. When he left I told them that he would ask for their souls to play with him. Sure enough, on his next visit he did just that! I had prepared my husband and he knew what to do. He was turned down and asked to leave. This caused the band to split up because the other band members thought that it was a joke and that I was just crazy. Satan tried to use this to turn my husband against me. God had prepared me to stand up to satan and rebuke him from our home. The flier I had begun with had become a booklet of several pages. It is hard to explain the feeling at this time, the word awesome is not even close. I was frightening my family. I was talking about the better world that would soon be here. Everything is going to be perfect the way it was in the beginning. On my birthday August 6, 1996 my husband called my parents. They came and called an ambulance and I was taken to the ER. My blood pressure was sky high, 230/120. I didn't have insurance at that time so they got my blood pressure down and sent me home. No tests of any kind was run. I was talking out of my head and very hot. My husband and son took turns all night trying to cool my head. Jeff, took me to the doctor the next day. They referred me to the emergency room in Birmingham. Once there I was admitted to the mental ward and never checked for anything linked to high blood pressure. They told my family I would be there for a long time. I do not have a history or a family history of mental illness. I do have a history of HBP. I had been on disability a few months because of my uncontrollable high blood pressure. While in BMC, my sister-in-law Shelia entered my song Beware in a poem contest. It won 3rd place and was published in the poem book--"Whisper's in the Garden" by the Poetry Guild. I was surprised when they told me. But of course, I didn't write it for it was given to me as a gift.

I don't remember much of the time at BMC. They kept trying to knock me out with meds, but I kept right on talking. They kept me for 7 days and with God's help I made them let me go on the 7th night. I was still talking out of my head. They gave me Lithium 900mgs and stelazine 20mgs daily. They knocked me out for 5 weeks. I couldn't hardly move, I couldn't eat, I couldn't do anything. They wheeled me into the Dr.'s office in a wheelchair. He apologized and told us that it was side effects of the stelazine. It had brought me down physically. He said to stop taking it immediately, and to take benadryl to get it out of my system. I came home and began to recover. He told my parents I was bipolar and manic depressive, which are mental diseases. He kept me on lithium 900 mgs daily. Satan wanted me sedated and my family frightened where I'd be quiet. I was back to normal except for the tireness of the meds. I wasn't allowed to mention God in anyway, shape or form. I had another "episode" in Dec. 1996 and again in Jan. 1997. Each time I told of the better world we were living in. The world God meant it to be. In Jan. 1997 the Dr. didn't have an appointment until March 24th. Maybe this was due to the fact I didn't have money for the payment and I still owed for earlier treatment. He told my mom on the phone without seeing me to give me the stelazine again, after knowing what it had done to me before. I knew what it had done so I wouldn't take it. They fed it to me in my food, without my knowledge. Of course, it brought me down physically again. They didn't know what to do with me since the Dr. couldn't see me until March. Mom called Cheaha Mental Health Center. They told her since I didn't have insurance the best place for me would be Byrics State Hospital. They set up a court date, had me picked up by the county police and taken to court. I told them in court that it was the meds, which they fed to me in my food, but no one would listen. I told them the Dr. had taken me off them before because of side effects. To no avail, I was sentenced to Byrics for 150 days. I was not even allowed to tell Jeff goodbye. I breaks my heart recalling being in the back of a cop car, both of our hands pressed on the window, crying out to each other and not being able to touch one another. Once I arrived at Byrics, I kept telling them I didn't belong there, that it was the meds. They gave me a foreign Dr. that didn't even acknowledge God. They discontinued the meds and brought my blood pressure under control. After being under such circumstances it was sky high. The only reason I didn't die during all this misdiagnosis and stress is God's grace and purpose he has for my life. They change my meds even though I had no symptoms. After 2 months of passing mental tests, they couldn't find anything wrong with me so they released me. They kept talking to me about low self-esteem due to the fact I kept telling them my husband comes first. I was told I should think of myself first, but God's word tells us God first then your spouse not yourself. So, I refused to do that. They diagnosed me as psychotic NOS, which means not otherwise specified. In other words, they didn't know what had caused me to talk out of my head. They just knew that I didn't have any symptoms the entire time I was there. While I was there a nurse told me that lithium wasn't to be given without weekly blood test. It can buildup a toxic level in your blood stream. I had been on it for 6 months without a single blood test. After returning home, I wasn't allowed to discuss God again. This was exactly what Satan had planned. He tried several ways to kill me and God wouldn't allow it so he used my families fear that I would become "sick" again to silence me for over 2 years. In Dec. 1998 my grandfather had a stroke. He talked out of his head and was very hot. Dr.'s knew right away he had a stroke. He had several more strokes during his week stay in the hospital. You see there are two types of strokes. A physical stroke that causes damage you can see and a mental stroke that shows no physical damage. The latter is what my grandfather and I had. He died Dec. 7th, 1998. If it wasn't for his strokes enlightening me of the facts, I would have never been tested for a stroke and I would have never known I wasn't so called "sick". I went to a neurologist and requested him to run test for a stroke. He ran an MRI and confirmed that I had had several light strokes. So each time I had an "episode", I actually had a stroke instead. He also said my blood was so thick; I could have had another stroke at anytime. He started me on blood thinner immediately. I also found out that I was a diabetic, which with the high blood pressure contributed to cause the strokes. It's shameful in this modern day medical times that these factors were overlooked and I spent years of agony misdiagnosed as "mentally ill". Without these findings, if I had had another stroke, they would have locked me back up in Byrics or I would have died. I believe in my heart, during those times, I was walking in the spirit and God held me in his arms and kept me safe and blessed me with no visible stroke damage. You see God has other plans for me and I will follow his will and let him guide me to finish whatever he wants me to do. God gave me these things I have written as a gift of wisdom and knowledge to share with everyone who will listen. The message is now!! The message is urgent!! Jesus is coming sooner than you think!

Now as I stated earlier, at BMC I was heavily sedated. As I told you before, I was talking out of my head and the things I talked about were of God and the last days. I purchased my records and they claimed my conversations were bizarre. Before I share some of the things I said in the records you must understand I was brought up Church of Christ and I didn't know most of the terms or actions I used. I had also not attended church in over 20 years. At one point I read that I tried to "heal" a fellow patient of his "Cane affliction" by "laying on of hand". They must have meant "Cain affliction" . I assume that this man must have been a murder, because Cain was the world's first murder. I feel the knowledge and wisdom I possess is God sent. For as it tells in Galations 1:12 I did not receive it from any man nor was taught it; rather I received it by revelation from Jesus Christ. After reviewing everything that happened to me; having strokes, not being treated for them instead being given heavy antipsychotic,being kept very upset being locked away from my husband and family and not being checked for diabetes, I probably should have died. That's what Satan wanted. He didn't get that so he tried to discredit my wisdom and knowledge by being labeled a "mental patient" and that didn't happen either. Then he tried using God's word against me because I am a woman. That doesn't work either! God knew who I was when he called me to do his work. By God's grace and loving care I'm still here and going strong doing God's will. I'm very thankful to God for

keeping me safe and giving me the opportunity to serve him with all my heart, all my soul and all my might in these last days. Hopefully, you will join me in the fight in these last days in which we are living! *THANK YOU JESUS!!!*

SEEK THE KINGDOM FIRST

Do any of these things sound familiar to you? Does your life fall into this pattern? Unsuccessful at everything you put your hand to. Things look good for a while then the bottom seems to fall out. Ever made the statement "If it wasn't for bad luck I'd have no luck at all". Well, surprise, forget about luck, your life is made up of your own choices. You unconsciously, without knowing the truth, have chosen to be miserable, unhappy, sick, and oppressed. It's time you dusted off your owner's manual, the BIBLE, and learn why you're here, how to become successful, how to be healthy, and how to be happy while you're still here. If you're miserable here without JESUS, what will your eternity be like? And if you think, well being saved is all my business. I'm not hurting anyone else, your sadly mistaken! Read Numbers 14:18 and Duet. 28:59.

Today everyone is seeking the answers to why America's children are behaving in the manner of terrorist in our society. With all of America's politics, socialist, psychics, lawmakers, doctors, and anti-Christian beliefs you have created this Godless society in which we're living today, which supposed to be progress. Generations of children brought up without morals. Never taught the "GOLDEN RULE" instead they learned the "GREED RULE" ----Do unto others before they do unto you. What's the matter, aren't you proud of what you have given your children. You've taught them that material items are more important than them. What do I mean by such a statement. Well, do you put your job ahead of your family? Does the almighty dollar rule in your home? Do you spend time with your children or pay them to get lost so they'll be out of your hair for the small time your not working? This country thinks it's so advanced and so great but look at your lives. Ask yourself what is so important, you think you want to give your children everything you didn't have right? Maybe you should stop and think your children may want something you did have instead! Well, what could that be? Try family time, togetherness, good old fashion LOVE. Love is more important than any amount of money! All the money in the world can't make you happy without love. Today's children are begging and pleading to be loved. So why not give them what they need which is your time not your money. If you were told your child was dieing wouldn't you try to save them? They're already dead in sin---for sin causes death. If your child were in jail you would spare no expense to have them released, but their prisoners already. If your child was sick you would seek the best care---but prayer is the last resort after all else fails! If your child don't respect you wouldn't that upset you? They don't most of the time because they do not Honor your father and mother. If someone was out to harm your child wouldn't you want to protect them? Their on Satan's #1 hit list, but you do not plead the blood of Jesus for them. If you were told your child could have many blessings and have all their needs meet, wouldn't you seek for it? But you've never taught them to choose the blessings over the curse. If you were told your child could have immortality wouldn't you try to find it. You never taught them to call on the name of JESUS and receive the free gift of grace. What's wrong with parent's today? Most parents claim to love their children. They want them to have the best of everything. They sometimes work long hours to provide them with the things they didn't have. They start when they're young to provide for the best of man's worldly knowledge of education. They want them to have the best of man's health insurance. But they leave out the most important thing---GOD's life insurance. You know "eternal" life insurance. A cost free gift that most of today's children have been denied. The last few generations created this moralless society that we live in today. Lovers of themselves and money. Thinking only of their selves, living for the "Father of I Wills". Their children have the best clothes, shoes, homes, cars, education, jobs, and social life. But their not providing them with the best future as they may think. The future is eternal. If you put a price on immortality they would pay any price---but it's a free gift they don't even acknowledge, because of their learned behavior of past generations. What good will it be for a man if he gains the whole world yet forfeits his soul? Most of today's children do not know these things. They don't know who the real enemy is! They don't know of the unseen treasures. They don't know these are the last days. They need to be taught how to be warriors. They need discipline. If your child dislikes work read them II Thess. 3:10. When your child comes home wanting a tattoo or body piercing ---what's your reply? When they ask why not just read them Leviticus 19:28. Not I said so but GOD says so! When your child wants to call a psychic--what's your reply? When they ask why not read them Lev. 26:31, 20:6 and Deut. 18:10 not because I said so but because GOD say so! When we sit our children down to have the sex talk, please begin with GOD's way and not the world's view. Not safe sex but abstainance. The world says this is not a working way for children. GOD says it's the only way. Don't just tell them don't do it. Explain to them why. The joining together as one is a marriage blood covenant. There are only two blood covenants in the bible. The first is the blood covenant of the church and the second is marriage. This union is very important in the eyes of GOD. Read them Mark 10:6-9 pertaining to becoming one flesh. So when you join together you become one. This means your spirits join also. You need to stop and think what spirit are you joining with. This can also be used in warning about unions with Christians and an unsaved partner. Deut. Tells us sin causes death. Joining together out of marriage causes all kinds of std's including the ones that kill. What does is tell us, sin causes death, the same yesterday, today, and forever. Explain to our children how the enemy will plant the thoughts of impurities but you must plant GOD's seed of thought with the truth of the beauty of joining in marriage. The knowledge of the blood covenant and how beautiful GOD's way can be. Read Ephesians 5:31 and II Tim 2:2. If we tell our children these truths; then waiting till marriage will become important to them. Not just a rule to break. Joining as one will have great meaning for them as it should be. You may also want them to read Proverbs 31:10 pertaining to a Noble Wife. And Proverbs 5 & 6:20-29; Proverbs 7. Let's get united together as Christians and take our stand for our beliefs in GOD. We're all to reach unity in the faith and knowledge and become mature, attaining to the whole measure of the fullness of Christ. The times have reached their fulfillment to bring all things in heaven and on earth together under one head, CHRIST JESUS OUR LORD AND SAVIOR. It's time to be like Acts 4:32. All believers were one in heart and mind. It tells in Luke 11:17 any kingdom divided won't stand. So it's time to stop quarrelling about words and all Christians unite in GOD's will. It's time to join together and as it tells us in II Tim. Come endure hardship with us like a good soldier of Christ Jesus. If GOD asked "What have you done for me lately?" what would your answer be today? Would he answer "well done my good and faithful servant" or would his reply be "WELL?". It's time to get back to the morals of yesterday---when our forefathers built the foundation of this country on GOD's Word. It's time to get serious about GOD's work! It's time to get right or get left!!!! We're to prepare GOD's people for works of service so that the body of Christ maybe built up! Put on your armor! Let's fight!!!!!

BLESSING OR CURSE

Now, at some time or another you have probably asked yourself why am I here? Why does this or that happen to me? Well, if you've never found the answer to these questions, you've been looking in the wrong places. It is very surprising just how simple the answers are to these questions. It's so easy. The answers are written clearly in black and white. But it's human nature to try and complicate everything. GOD said: See I am setting before you today a blessing and a curse--- the blessing if you obey the commands of the Lord your GOD that I am giving you today; the curse if you disobey the commands of the Lord your GOD and turn from the way that I command you today by following other gods which you have not known. GOD is the same yesterday, today and forever. And so is his word. Is your god the almighty dollar, your job, your possessions, or yourself? Are you living the blessing or the curse? It's all your choice. You are to rejoice before the Lord your GOD in everything you put your hand to. Be sure to set aside a tenth of all you produce. Are you robbing GOD of tithes and offerings? You should seek the kingdom first. GOD's money comes first before anything else. If you don't have the money then something has come before GOD right? GOD tells us prove me. You can't out give GOD. He will always give more back than you can give. Try it some times. GOD tells there should be no poor among you, for in the land the Lord you GOD is giving you to posses as your inheritance he will richly bless you, if only you fully obey the Lord your GOD and be careful to follow all his commands. Let no one be found among you who sacrifices his son or daughter in the fire, who practices divination or sorcery, interprets omens, engages in witchcraft or cast spells, or who consults the dead. Love the Lord your GOD and walk always in his ways. Whatever your lips utter you must be sure to do because you made your vow freely to the Lord your GOD with your own mouth. The Lord your GOD detests anyone who deals dishonestly. If you fully obey the Lord your GOD and carefully follow all his commands, he will set you high above all the nations on earth. The Lord will send a blessing on everything you put your hand to. The Lord will open the heavens, the storehouse of his bounty, to send rain on your land in season and to bless all the work of your hands. You will lend and not borrow. The Lord will make you the head, not the tail. If you pay attention to the commands of the Lord your GOD and carefully follow them you will always be at the top, never at the bottom. However, if you do not obey the Lord your GOD and do not carefully follow all his commands and decrees, all these curses will come upon you and your kneading trough will be cursed. The fruit of your womb will be cursed and the crops of your land and the calves of your herds and the lambs of your flocks will be cursed. You will be cursed when you come in and cursed when you go out. The Lord will send on you curses, confusion and rebuke in everything you put your hand to, until you are destroyed and come to sudden ruin because of the evil you have done in forsaking him. The Lord will plague you with diseases until he has destroyed you. The Lord will strike you with wasting disease with fever and inflammation with scorching heat and drought with blight and mildew, which will plague you until you perish. The Lord will cause you to be defeated before your enemies. You will be unsuccessful in everything you do; day after day you will be oppressed and robbed with no one to rescue you! You will be pledged to be married to a woman but another will take her and ravish her. You will build a house but you will not live in it. You will plant a vineyard but you will not even begin to enjoy its fruit. You will have sons and daughters but you will not keep them because they will go into captivity. Because you did not serve the Lord your GOD joyfully and gladly in the time of prosperity, therefore in hunger and thirst, in nakedness and dire poverty, you will serve the enemies the Lord sends against you. The Lord is slow to anger, abounding in love and forgiving sin and rebellion. Yet he does not leave the guilty unpunished; he punishes the children for the sin of the fathers to the third and forth generations. If you do not carefully follow all the words of his law which are written in his book and do not revere his glorious and awesome name---the Lord your GOD---the Lord will send fearful plagues on you and your descendants, harsh and prolonged disasters and severe and lingering illnesses. He will bring upon you all the diseases of Egypt that you dreaded and they will cling to you. The Lord will also bring on you every kind of sickness and disaster not recorded in his Book of the Law, until you are destroyed. Just as it pleased the Lord to make you prosper and increase in number, so it will please him to ruin and destroy you. The Lord will give you an anxious mind, eyes weary with longing and a despairing heart. You will live in constant suspense filled with dread both night and day, never sure of your life. Do any of these things ring a bell in your life? Have you ever thought about your living a curse caused by your own choices? GOD's not a liar so it's time you start thinking about the choices in your life and the consequences of your actions! When you and your children return to the Lord your GOD and obey him with all your heart and with all your soul according to everything he commands you, then the Lord your GOD will restore your fortunes and have compassion on you. The Lord will again delight in you and make you prosperous, just as he delighted in your fathers. See he sets before you today life and prosperity; death and destruction. But the choice is all yours. Now choose life, so that you and your children may live and that you may love the Lord your GOD, listen to his voice, and hold fast to him. So, see your purpose here is to serve the Lord and obey his commands and to win souls for JESUS. The answer to why things happen is above and all are your free choices. So please today choose the blessing over the curse. See Christ hath redeemed us from the curse of the law, being made a curse for us....for it is written, Cursed is everyone that hangeth on a tree: That the blessing of Abraham might come on the Gentiles through JESUS CHRIST; that we might receive the promise of the Spirit through faith (Galations 3:13-14). So dear friends if you don't have JESUS as your Savior you are living the curse. If you're tired of living a life where every time things get to looking better, then bam something bad happens. Turn to JESUS! He is the answer. Please don't wait till a disaster befalls you before you call on JESUS. Learn how to live in this life successfully while you're here. You know no one is promised his or her next breath. Life is short, why not make the best of it by accepting all of GOD's promises.

KNOW WHO YOU ARE!

Please turn to (read) II Timothy 3:1-5 Now isn't this like most of today's "religion"----having a form of godliness but denying its power. These people honor GOD with their lips but their hearts are far from him. They worship him in vain, their teachings are but rules taught by men. JESUS was crucified through weakness yet he lives by GOD's power. Likewise we are weak in him yet by GOD's power we will live with him to serve GOD. So do not think your in the least inferior to these "super-apostles". You may not be a trained speaker, but you do have knowledge. For you did not receive a spirit that makes you a slave again to fear but you received the spirit of sonship and by him we cry "Abba Father". The spirit himself testifies with our spirit that we are GOD's children. Now if we are children then we are heirs---heirs of GOD and Co-heirs with Christ if indeed we share in his sufferings in order that we may also share in his glory. So you are no longer a slave but a son and since you are a son, GOD has made you also an heir. It is for freedom that Christ has set us free. Stand firm then and do not let yourselves be burdened again by a yoke of slavery. And we know that in all things GOD works for the good of those who love him who have been called according to his purpose. For those GOD foreknew he also predestined to be conformed to the likeness of his son that he might be the firstborn among many brothers. And those he predestined, he also called, those he called he also justified, those he justified he also glorified. He raised you up for this very purpose that you might display his power in you, that his name might be proclaimed in all the earth. We have different gifts according to the grace given us. So then, men ought to regard us as servants of Christ and as entrusted with the secret of GOD. He will bring to light what is hidden in darkness and will expose the motives of men's hearts. For this world in it's present form is passing away. So we fix our eyes not on what is seen but on what is unseen.

For what is seen is temporary but what is unseen is eternal. For though we live in the world we do not wage war as the world does. For this war is not of flesh and blood. The weapons we fight with are not weapons of the world. On the contrary, they have divine power to demolish strongholds. So, set your minds on things above not on earthly things. In JESUS we have redemption, through his blood we have forgiveness of sins, in accordance with the riches of GOD's grace that he lavished on us with all wisdom and understanding. And he made known to us the mystery of his will according to his good pleasure which he purposed in Christ to put into effect, when the times will have reached their fulfillment to bring all things in heaven and on earth together under one head even Christ. In him we were also chosen having been predestined according to the plan of him who works out everything in conformity with the purpose of his will. I pray that the eyes of your heart be enlightened in order that you may know the hope to which he has called you, the riches of his glorious inheritance in the saints and his incomparably great power for us who believe. For it is by grace you have been saved through faith and this is not from yourselves it is the gift of GOD, not by works so that no one can boast. For it is light that makes everything visible. Because the days are evil. Watch out for those dogs, those men who do evil, many live as enemies of the cross of Christ. Their destiny is destruction. Their mind is on earthly things. Whatever you have learned or received put it into practice. GOD will meet all your needs according to his glorious riches in Christ JESUS. My purpose is that they may be encouraged in heart and united in love so that they may have the full riches of complete understanding in order that they may know the mystery of GOD namely Christ in whom are hidden all the treasures of wisdom and knowledge. And whatever you do whether in word or deed do it all in the name of the Lord JESUS giving thanks to GOD the father through him. Devote yourselves to prayer being watchful and thankful. Do not put out the spirits fire. Do not treat prophecies with contempt. Test everything. Hold on to the good. Avoid every kind of evil. The Lord is faithful and he will strengthen and protect you from the evil one. I remind you to fan into flame the gift of GOD. Guard the good deposit that was entrusted to you. Guard it with the help of the Holy Spirit who lives in us. Be strong in the grace that is in Christ JESUS. Therefore prepare your minds for action, be self-controlled so that you can pray. Be merciful to those who doubt, snatch others from the fire and save them, to others show mercy. Do not worry about how you will defend yourselves or what you will say for the Holy Spirit will teach you at that time, what you should say. Do not be afraid. Keep on speaking. Do not be silent. For JESUS is with you and no one is going to attack and harm you. For no weapon forged against you will prosper. If we are out of our mind it is for the sake of GOD. There is nothing concealed that will not be disclosed or hidden that will not be made known. Show proper respect to everyone. Do not take revenge my friends but leave room for GOD's wrath for it is written: It is mine to avenge, I will repay says the Lord. In your anger do not sin. Do not let the sun go down while you're still angry and do not give the devil a foothold. And when you stand praying if you hold anything against anyone forgive him so that your Father in heaven may forgive you your sins. You also must be ready because the Son of Man will come at an hour when you do not expect him.

Outside are the dogs those who loves and practice magic arts, the sexually immoral, the murders, the idolaters and everyone who loves and practices falsehood. Therefore keep watch because you do not know the day or hour. No one knows about the day or hour, not even the angels in heaven, nor the Son, but only the Father. Be on guard! Be alert! You do not know when that time will come. But he did give the signs of the last days and we're living in them today. JESUS tells us, I tell you the truth, this generation will certainly not pass away until all these things have happened. And you will see the Son of Man sitting at the right hand of the Mighty One and coming on the clouds of heaven. For the Son of Man in his day will be like the lightening which flashes and lights up the sky from one end to the other. Just as it was in the days of Noah, so also will it be in the days of the Son of Man. Whoever tries to keep his life will lose it and whoever loses his life will preserve it. Today, if you hear his voice do not harden your hearts. Come endure hardship with us like a good soldier of Christ JESUS!!

LEARN TO CONTROL OUR BIG MOUTHS

In the beginning GOD's spoken word created our very world in which we live. GOD has used man to speak his plans into existence since the beginning. It tells us that our tongues have the power of life and death. Our mouths are compared to rudders on a ship. Has your mouth shipwrecked you on life's sea? Speak life into your life, not death. Are you guilty of telling everyone how sick you always feel, or maybe how miserable you are, or how about how broke you stay? It also tells our words boast of great things. Our tongues are small but like a tiny spark they can do great damage. Think back in your lives. Is your life turning out the way you have said it would be? How about your children? Do you always tell them positive or negative things? Your tongue shapes your life and your children's lives. So isn't it time you learn to tame your tongue. We're told to bridle our mouths like a horse wears a bit. That small bridle in a horse's mouth can guide a huge horse, so likewise we need to bridle our mouth's to guide our lives. This can only be accomplished with the help of the Holy Spirit. GOD also tells us if we do not bridle our tongue it will delude our own hearts and our service is worthless. Out of abundance of the heart the mouth speaks. Your words are like seeds in your lives. What you sow will come up! Speak things into your life that can be backed up by the word of GOD. Remember, we're created in GOD's image so we're to act like him. So GOD's mighty word of power is to be used in our lives today. Speak GOD's promises out of our mouths and bring them into existence. It tells us our words are justified and they also condemn. The written word of GOD is his formal decree. So get GOD's word in your heart and begin declaring it out of your mouth. We're told to confess with our mouths, this confirms salvation before men and confirms your position before the enemy of your soul. It tells us to speak to the mountain and it will move. What are some of the mountains in your life?

Do you speak at them or about them? It's time to learn the difference! Start moving your mountains to the side, instead of climbing up them. We're to think smarter not harder. Stand up and learn the power of your mouth. Put it to good use instead of damning your situations. Do you know when you constantly do that you are putting a curse on what you're speaking about? We're told to guard our mouths and tongue. He who guards his mouth keeps his life. As Christians we are sealed in the Holy Spirit. Think of yourself as a slice of bread in a ziplock bag. That bread is fresh as long as the bag is sealed. If you break the seal the bread becomes stale. The same way you become without the Holy Spirit. Before you except JESUS as your Savior and the Holy Spirit lives in you, your heart is as hard as that piece of stale bread. Soften up and get a fresh start in your lives. Learn to love one another and speak the truth of love. Change your life with words of love and change the lives of others around you. Remember, be careful of the words you speak! It could mean your life!!!

DIVINE DELIVERANCE

Get your glasses adjusted, you old skeptics and old doubters, bless your hearts we're going to shake you over hell with the word of GOD Almighty. Let's turn this old world upside down. The Bible tells us that He is able to do exceedingly abundantly above all that we ask or think, according to the power that worketh in us. Now that's the thing to believe if you want victory. There isn't anything that you would withhold from your children. We love our children and because we love them, we give. Our heavenly Father also gives to us, his children. He tells us that He will not withhold anything good from them that walk uprightly. GOD loves us with a tremendous love that has never been fathomed by the mind of man. Now faith comes by hearing and hearing by the Word of

GOD. We save for our earthly children and leave for them an inheritance. Our heavenly Father loves us so much he gave his only begotten Son, where we could tap into our heavenly inheritance. Divine healing is the heritage of the Church of JESUS Christ. This is one of the sweetest blessings ever given to mankind and only the tip of the iceberg when it comes to GOD's promises for his children. Peter tells us by his stripes we were healed. We're also told that beloved I wish above all things that thou prosperth and be in health, even as thou soul prosperth. So do you believe the BIBLE! You have to know these promises before you can reach out and grab them. JESUS tells us my people perish for lack of knowledge. Dust off your bibles; learn GOD's will and promises. GOD tells us to come and do his will. JESUS bore our sickness, carried our diseases and forgave our sins. Without the shedding of blood, there is no remission for sin. Without the stripes on his back, there is no divine healing for a fallen race. Our deliverance for soul and body comes from Christ that died on the cross that we might be saved and healed. It is the will of GOD that everybody be healed, who will believe. So what is the salvation of a sick man? To get well! Salvation to the sinner is being delivered from his sins. This truth is the power of GOD unto salvation. It works!! You are healed just like you are saved through the atoning grace of GOD. GOD has made provision, not only for the salvation of the soul, but for the body of man also. Ye shall know the truth and the truth shall make you free. Free from sickness, free from sin. Both must come by faith. All hell can't keep miracles from being manifested where faith is exercised. GOD's way is not coercion, but His way is "Whosoever will let him come". You are a believer when you stand alone on the word of GOD. As faith rises in your heart then you will receive your healing. GOD's mighty power and your faith will make you whole. We have the Holy Spirit and it tells us He will abide with us forever. He is the miracle worker through those who believe. The power of the Holy Spirit will set you free. We have to drive doubt and fear from our hearts and lives. Believe in GOD and he will set you free. Look unto JESUS the author and finisher of our faith. Faith is a powerful weapon in the hands of anyone who will use it. Believe with all your heart that whatsoever you ask in the name of JESUS that it is done! Compare this faith to the hope of the second coming of Christ. A power that will bring deliverance to a suffering world. Put the joy of the Lord in your heart. That will make you a living person that will bring life, happiness, sunshine and joy to the world that you shake hands with from day to day. GOD wants men and women empowered with the Holy Spirit to carry the message to the lost and dying world today. This is no new revelation, just a more perfect illumination. Except your double portion of GOD's spirit that he is pouring out in abundance in these last days.

What the world needs to do and what the church needs to do is to place their faith in an infallible GOD and simply believe the Bible when it says: JESUS CHRIST IS THE SAME YESTERDAY, TODAY AND FOREVER. Don't look unto yourselves or worldly wisdom and understanding and think that that is going to get you through. Look to the living Christ. The Light of the World, the Bread of Life, the Lamb of GOD. How can anyone doubt that JESUS CHRIST heals the sick today? You do not get anything until you BELIEVE! Most people today have frosty cold hearts, turned away from the power of GOD and accepted a form of Godliness but deny the power thereof. Results are they no longer bring forth children into the kingdom of GOD. Count the promises of GOD sure, steadfast and unmovable and they will be brought to pass in perfect fulfillment in your life, if you stand on the Rock of the Word of the living GOD. It's time for dominations to stop quibbling over words and get into the Word for we're all GOD's children. Join together in unity and seek that heartfelt religion that moves your heart and quickens your mortal body. Let's all be of one heart, one mind and one accord. For our goal is the same. Put life back into your poor old dry hides that never feel anything, never sees anything or that never finds out very much. Let the spirit spark new life in your soul as it raised JESUS from the dead. Reach out, step over the line and take it by faith! Don't get discouraged when somebody criticizes you. You have to answer the critic once in a while. You have to put them in their place. JESUS had critics, too. Most of His trouble came from the church crowd. Same as today. They say "that is done away with....there is nothing to it anymore." Now we're talking about healing, miracles and demon-spirits. They told the people that JESUS was doing those things by the spirit of Beelzebub.

Get ready you may hear those same words. But our reply should be the same as JESUS' was in his day. "All manner of sin and blasphemy shall be forgiven unto me, but the blasphemy against the Holy Spirit shall not be forgiven unto men." When JESUS set the man possessed with a legion of devils free a bunch of hypocrites complained and sought to run JESUS out of town. A great number of demons had that one man bound, but Christ came and set him free. Today, people are bound in this same way. Everyone is looking for explanations for the recent rash of killings. Especially from the youth of today. These things are written as the signs of the last days. The days in which we're living today. Hello, Wake Up, dust off your Bibles. Stop perishing from lack of knowledge!! This godless society has created these "little demons", called the children doing these horrible acts. Most of these acts of terrorisms done on their peers and even family members are done for seemly no apparent reasons. Experts sometimes try to explain it by bad experiences, causing mental stress or mental illness....JESUS called it demon-possession or to put it mildly demon influenced. Show me scripture where JESUS told us that when he went away that there would be no healings, no miracles, and that he bound all the demons of hell already and we wouldn't have to deal with them anymore. There is none. Instead, he tells that when he left he would send us a comforter. The Holy Spirit, which will be with us forever. When Christ's Church, which is us believer's leaves so will the Holy Spirit. JESUS also tells us John 14:12 "I tell you the truth anyone who has faith in me will do what I have been doing. He will do even greater things than these. Luke 10:19 tells that he gives us authority to overcome all the power of the enemy; nothing will harm you. II Thess. 3:3 But the Lord is faithful and he will strengthen and protect you from the evil one. Now I've given you several scriptures but the main one is JESUS is the same yesterday, today and forever. Give me one scripture saying different. Well, GOD's not a lair. So it all comes down to do you believe GOD's word or not. Faith brings results. You see I can say these things because it is GOD's Word. Not a man's opinion. Healing is for you. He will heal you today, just as he healed those back then. There's nothing to fear. GOD has made you free. He is the answer for the problems of today. He does say also "Sin no more, lest a worse thing come unto thee."

So let's cast all our cares upon JESUS; our sorrows, headaches, afflictions and diseases. He will give you rest. Be made whole. What do you have to lose? Just try him. Oh, world of modern day skeptics, atheists, infidels, doctors of theology, new agers and so on...the word of GOD is a lion. Just turn it loose and it will defend itself! It is not something new, it is the Glory of GOD, and has been utilized by every faithful Saint, every faithful prophet, every preacher and is still used by the people who believe and live true to the living GOD. The time has come for the old-time, bloodbought, Holy Spirit, miracle-working GOD sent revival with power to save the world, heal the sick and set the captives free. Get your eyes on JESUS!!! Faith is the substance we want. If you say if I see then I'll believe, that's not faith. You're looking to circumstances symptoms, etc. Come on you bunch of modern day doubting Thomas'. You half-heartily ask for prayer, then crack an eye, peep around and see if anything happens and say if I receive my healing, then I'll believe. GOD bless you, if you come with that attitude you'll never get well. We must believe GOD's word is truth. We must believe, all things are possible to him that believeth. This kind of faith will be the turning point in your sick, sinful, disappointed lives. When we get to the place that we can believe in this power and place our confidence in Him and have a faith that holds no doubt; Healing will be ours. JESUS says, "It is not if I can or if I will but if thou will believe". This is the power of faith! Believe GOD and His Word!! You'll not be disappointed. Don't look unto a church. Don't look unto any man. Just look unto JESUS!!!!!!!! JESUS is the name above all names. The King of Kings and Lord of Lords. The Lamb of GOD. The Lion of the tribe of Judah. The healer of all the sick. The savior of all sinners. He's the great Sheppard of our souls. The very pillow and foundation of our faith. Now, if you want faith, draw nigh to GOD. Everything that you need in life can be found in JESUS CHRIST. The power of hell may assail. The circumstances may hinder, but it is when your eyes are on Christ that you cannot go down. He is a wonderful JESUS! So you dare to reach out to believe the promises of GOD on unstoppable faith? Then put GOD first in your life and step back, watch the storehouse of heaven open for you. We are already given. We just need to claim our inheritance. You have not, for you ask not. We limit GOD. We have so much doubt and fear in our hearts, that GOD can't do anything for us. Take him at his word. Come boldly to the throne of grace. Place your finger on His Word and say "Father it is promised here, and I come to claim it from the Book of Life. I thank you for it, Loving GOD....In the name of JESUS CHRIST. He wants you to be happy. He wants you to be victorious. He holds it all in His hands and He has promised to give it to His children if they will only believe Him. He lifts His children from a world of darkness into a kingdom of Love and marvelous light! We have riches untold! Let's quit feeling sorry for ourselves and trust in Him who never fails! We cannot fail unless we quit! I hope this is settling down in your heart and sets it a blaze. Become on fire for JESUS! We need the love of GOD in our hearts. Today, what stands in your way of the promises? What's so important to you that it's worth eternal hell for!! What is your excuse? Not ready yet!! Look at the things you are missing. Dear friends, you're not promised your next breath. Don't be caught dead without JESUS CHRIST, our Lord and Savior. We're living under GOD's mercy now. We're living in the day of Grace; in a day when GOD is trying to reach you. He is a GOD of Love and Compassion. He is a GOD of feeling and of course He will be a GOD of Anger yet to be faced by a Christ-rejecting world. Please except his wonderful gift of grace and take hold of his promises and love. Bow now or bow later! The choice is yours. The choice is now.

IT'S NOT ABOUT RELIGION!

Religion is defined as the adherence to a set of beliefs that regulate the moral, social and ritualistic behavior of a individual. Everyone on earth is religious in some kind of form because religion is the result of an inherent hunger in the human spirit that man cannot define yet must seek to satisfy. Religion is a natural phenomenon that has existed in some form in every human culture. Every major problem in history and in our contempory world can be traced to some religious foundation. All oppressive practices have been justified by some kind of religious code or system. Religion is the very thing by its nature is supposed to provide the solution to mankind's problems and provide hope and faith for life but instead has created more problems throughout history than it has solved. Everyone looks for the meaning for their existence and the power to control their lives and circumstances. Our pursuit of purpose and power is the primary source and motivation for the development of religion. Rather than uniting humanity with common power and knowledge of purpose, religion has proven itself instead to be the great divider of mankind. So, it is not about religion, it is about the reason for mankinds search for purpose and power. Man was created in GOD's image then given dominion over all the earth and over every creeping thing on earth(Genesis 1:26). Dominion is the purpose for man's creation and existence. Dominion can be translated as "kingdom" "sovereign rule" or "royal power". So mankind was created to have rulership over the earth. The first thing man was given by his Creator was a "kingdom". Dominion is the kingdom mandate that validates man's desire for power. It is also the foundation and source of man's need to control and rule his enviroment and circumstances. Power is natural to the human spirit. Mankind's failure through disobedience to his Creator resulted in the loss of his dominion over the earth and his gift of divine power but he did not lose Heaven.

So, mankind's search is not for a religion of for Heaven, but for his kingdom. This is why religion can never satisfy the deep hunger in the heart of man. No religion can substitute for the lost kingdom. Jesus' first announcement was the arrival of the kingdom of Heaven. His solution to the malnourished and bankrupt human spirit was not a religion but the Kingdom of Heaven. The Kingdom is GOD's priority and must become our priority if we are to overcome the confusion of religions and the threat of self-destruction. Religion preoccupies man until he finds the Kingdom. The Bible is about the establishment of a kingdom rulership on earth from Heaven through Mankind. It is about a royal family mandated to colonize earth from Heaven. This Kingdom assignment is the priority of GOD the Creator and the object of mankind's inherent pursuit. Everything Jesus said and did---His prayers, teachings, healings, and miracles---was focused on a kingdom, not a religion. The original intent of GOD's mandate to Moses was not to establish a religion but a nation of people who would love, serve, and honor GOD -- a "royal priesthood and a holy nation". Religion is one of the greatest obstacles to the Kingdom. Even Christianity as a religion, falls short of the message and concepts of the Kingdom of GOD. We must learn the difference between religion and the concept of the Kingdom of Heaven. Jesus Himself brought the Kingdom back to us. It was His main purpose in coming to earth in human flesh. We receive the Kingdom through His death. The Kingdom of Heaven is GOD's desire and purpose for us. GOD established only two priorites for mankind: the Kingdom of GOD and the righteouness of GOD. Kingdom refers to the governing influence of Heaven on earth and righteousness refers to right alignment and positioning with that government authority. GOD's plan for man was to extend His heavenly Kingdom (government) to the earth through the principle of colonization by His offspring, man. The kingdom was the first form of government on earth. Man was created for rulership, dominion and relationship with the Father. We are to be governed by the laws of heaven, led by GOD as our Heavenly King on earth. It's all about a King, a Kingdom and a royal family of children. A King has the power and can give it to whomever he chooses. He chose us through Jesus Christ. Jesus

Christ, is the ultimate Lord and owner of all things. GOD's original purpose and plan was to extend His invisible Kingdom of Heaven to earth through His offspring in His image--mankind--and to rule through man as a heavenly agency. A colony of Heaven on earth with man as GOD's delegated representatives. GOD's big picture is to extend His invisible rulership to this visible world. To have the relationship between the invisible realm of Heaven and the visible realm of earth. Connecting these two through colonization. The Bible, which is the constitution, lays out the laws, principles, and characteristics that define GOD's Kingdom. It is a government document that defines governmental intent and establishes governmental authority. Man, a Created being, is a spirit being after the nature and essence of the Creator, GOD the Father. He lives in a body, which is his earth suit that allows him to relate to the physical environment; and he possesses a soul, which is his intellect, will and emotional faculties. The earth is heaven's "crown land" and is personal property of the King. In a Kingdom the King owns everything, there is no such thing as private property. GOD owns the earth and everything on it; the earth is

His crown land which he has given to man. Crown land given to someone by the King remains crown land that he can take back at any time. So when he gave earth to man he did not relinquish ownership. He gave us rulership not ownership. Living on and using the land is a priviledge, not a right. The earth is Heaven's crown land and we are stewards of GOD's property. This is what it means to be a colony of Heaven. A colony is a group of emigrants or their descendants who settle in a distant land but remain subject to the parent country--GOD's purpose in colonizing earth was to show the spiritual powers of darkness how beings created in His own image could be planted on the earth and bring in the government and culture of Heaven so that in the end, the earth would look just like Heaven. GOD chose Earth as His Kingdom colony in the natural realm and placed on it human beings created in His image to run the colony for Him, which is merely an extension of His Kingdom in Heaven in the spiritual realm. He is the High King of Heaven who rules over human Kings He created to rule over the earthly domain. Adam and Eve's rebellion cost them their Kingdom, so GOD's plan is to restore what man lost which was a kingdom with rightful place as rulers of the earthly domain. The relationship between mankind and GOD the Father was broken also. The Cross of Christ is the doorway that gets us back in the Kingdom with restoration of power and authority for us in the name of Jesus Christ. Jesus also is a bridge for the broken relationship between the Father and mankind. It is regaining rulership on earth and a relationship with the Father as Children of GOD. Sons and daughters of the King serve as a priviledge not an obligation. In the Kingdom, the King's word is law. It is not open to debate, discussion, challenge, or amendment. So never give an opinion just GOD's word says it and that settles it, whether you or I believe it or not. The King's word is law and great reward follows obedience. Disobedience brings severe penalties. Jesus gives citizenship to His Kingdom for everyone who believes in Him-- --to everyone who accepts His message of the Kingdom. The good news of the gospel! That we are to go unto all the world and proclaim. JESUS proclaimed "Repent (change your mind and change your ways) for the Kingdom of Heaven is near(or has arrived). If you say "Jesus is Lord", you are acknowledging His authority over you as well as your responsibility to obey Him. If Jesus is Lord, He must receive first priority in your life. You cannot call Him Lord and then start making excuses for not obeying Him. You can't claim He owns you and do whatever you please. If Jesus is Lord, you can't live for Him one day a week or a few hours one day a week, while living for yourself the rest of the week. You must live a relationship everyday. Jesus is either Lord of all or He is not Lord at all. You choose to stay in the Kingdom of Darkness or accept Jesus the doorway to the Kingdom of Heaven, with all the rights as Kingdom citizens (which is children of GOD the Father). The most important confession any of us can make is to declare, "Jesus Christ is Lord". Then we can depend on Him for our welfare. For in a Kindgom the King provides for his citizens(his children). A King personally owns everything in his domain, citizens are granted the priviledge to use things in the kingdom. Submission, obedience, and thanksgiving is an acknowledgement of His lordship of your life. Living under a Lord means giving up all concepts of personal ownership which puts us into the position of full access to all of Heaven's resources. The King of Heaven has given us dominion authority here on earth, and He will not violate it without our permission. That means we're in charge here on earth. So we can't blame GOD for everything that goes wrong. GOD does not intervene because this is not His domain. Jesus gave dominion back to mankind before he returned to heaven. He gave us a comforter, that he told us will remain with us forever. He gave us authority to represent him here and we're to give him permission in earthly domain to intervene in affairs of those who hold dominion authority. That is why GOD needs Kingdom citizens to pray. Prayer is earthly license for Heavenly interferance. GOD works through the prayers of His people. The position and authority that Jesus won have been transferred back to mankind through spiritual rebirth in Christ. Though GOD is sovereign and all powerful He limited Himself concerning affairs of earth to working through us His representatives, His children. GOD didn't give away ownership of earth but he did assign responsibility of governing it to humanity. GOD has all power and authority yet, He has given mankind authority over the earth, as well as a free will and choice. He will not rescend those gifts. GOD needs human hands to heal, human voices to speak and human feet to go. Because of this dominion on earth, Christ had to come in human form to reclaim the Kingdom. If He had not come as a man, He would not have had the right to reclaim humanity and the earth for GOD according to the way GOD has ordered His purpose for the world. Jesus was the first born among many brothers.(Romans 8:29) The Word became flesh and made His dwelling among us.(John 1:14) In him we have redemption through his blood the forgiveness of sins in accordance with the riches of Gods' grace. Jesus delivered us legally. He voided Satan's contract over humanity breaking his dominion over us. He brought healing, set captives free, lifted oppression and liberated those under demonic control. Jesus fully accomplished the task of breaking the authority of Satan and voiding his legal hold upon the human race, someone on earth must represent Him in that victory and enforce it. It is our responsibility to enforce the victory as we also meet the powers of darkness. We through prayers of intercession meet the powers of darkness enforcing the victory in Christ. Through prayer we invite GOD to act in our domain. When we do,

Heaven invades our territory on our behalf. Prayer is essentially a partnership of the redeemed child of GOD working hand in hand with GOD toward the realization of His redemptive purposes on earth. The commission from GOD "Let them rule....overall the earth.(Gen 1:26) He has given His children His spirit so that we can agree with God's purposes even when we are uncertain about how to pray. Prayer is both a right and a privilege of redeemed man, who is now in a position to enter fully into a relationship of love with GOD and to agree that "His Kingdom come, His will be done on earth as it is in heaven".(Matt.6:10) So, you must change your mind and stop thinking like the world with it's inadequacies and start thinking like a Kingdom citizen! We are ambassadors of the Kingdom of Heaven. Ambassadors never gives their personal opinion; it's illegal. Kingdom citizens obey the laws of the King. Laws enforce and protect the standards by which the Kingdom operates. Regardless of what people think, the Bible is absolute truth and everything in it will work for our good if we obey it. GOD's laws are designed to prevent us from accepting and normalizing evil. Sin and violation have a ripple effect. These laws and principles are called by Jesus the "Keys of the Kingdom". Our "Keys" are called "Scriptures" and most of us don't know how to use them. Prayer is the key that opens the lock to the "warehouse" of Heaven--asking in Jesus' Name---according to His will and with His purpose. Freedom comes in knowing the truth. That is why Kingdom citizens can be confident in victory and success no matter what circumstances may suggest. In the world's system you get ahead any way you can. The Kingdom of Heaven operates on keys. It is the power of ignorance of Kingdom keys that can destroy us. The Kingdom of GOD is not a religion and citizenship is not a membership. The new birth makes us a naturalized citizen in the Kingdom of Heaven. We emigrated from a foreign country the "dominion of darkness". It returns us to our original "natural" state of authority and dominion over the earth as GOD intended from the start. The church(GOD children, Kingdom citizens) should be an embassy of His Kingdom--- a place where Kingdom citizens can receive aid, be trained in the ways, laws, language and customs of the Kingdom and be equipped with the Kingdom resources they need for effective life in the Kingdom Colony on earth. The Kingdom government exercises jurisdiction over us wherever we are. Our culture should reflect and reveal our citizenship as being here but not from here, as being in the world but not of the world. From this day forward, start living as GOD's child in His Kingdom, by His Kingdom principles. Let's rise to the occasion and embrace the incredible invitation to be co-labors with GOD to be carriers of His awesome Holy Spirit and ambassadors for His Kingdom. Let's represent Him!!!

PRAYER
AN EARTHLY LICENCE FOR HEAVENLY INTERFERENCE

Praying has different levels. There are different ways to pray. Daily praying should be as a conversation with GOD during your daily routines. Let him be in all your daily actitives. He likes to do even small things for his children. Things you would never have thought about asking for before. For example, on a trip to work or shopping ask for green lights, less traffic, good parking, good prices, people to be nice at work etc. Little things like these delight the Lord. But you need to pray for things alittle ahead of time, don't wait till you get in the parking lot to ask for a good parking place, ask before you arrive. He loves to do things for his children. He loves to be involved in your daily life.

Satan wants you to believe you shouldn't bother GOD with such small things. Remember Satan is a LAIR! Some things we need to petition GOD for. This means repeatedly. Sometimes our prayers are delayed or hindered. Sometimes we must wait on GOD's timing, sometimes prayers are hindered for different reasons. One of the things that can hinder prayer is holding something against someone. You must learn to turn the hurt loose and give it to GOD. Ask the Lord to take it from you. Forgive so that you may be forgiven. Prayers need to be out loud. Prayers need to be specific. Before praying think about how what you're asking will affect others. Always pray to the Father in JESUS name. Always believe your prayer will be answered with no doubt in your heart. Then don't be swayed in what is seen. Keep believing. There is also intercessory prayer. This is when we intercede for others or stand in the gap where they may fall short. A form of intercession releases the creative power or energy of the Holy Spirit into a situation to produce, create or give birth to something. GOD's will and timing needs someone on earth to birth it through prayer. Accompany asking with spiritual "warfare" or "wrestling" to enforce the victory of Calvary. Our ignorance of Satan and his tactics, as well as how to deal with them, is costly for us. The word "ignorant" means without knowledge or understanding. Satan makes a lot of gains on those who are unaware of his ways. He takes advantage of Christians unknowing of his schemes. Learn to be a Pro wrestler. Use praise as warfare. Attack the enemy. To ignore Satan is to abdicate to him. We must lift the veil off the mind of the unbeliever. The backbone of prayer is our agreement with God's Word, our oneness with Christ, who is the living Word and our unity with God's purpose and will. We are to pray to GOD as partners in His purposes. Prayer is joining forces with GOD the Father by calling attention to His promises. Prayer is essentially a partnership of the redeemed child of GOD toward the realization of His redemptive purposes on earth. If you are convinced that He will do what He has promised you, if you are pure both in what you believe and in what you do---then you will see Him manifested. Holiness is the key both to being persistent in prayer and to receiving answer to prayer. Holiness is being convinced that what GOD says and what GOD does are the same. Holiness means "one" in the sense of "complete". Holiness is telling the truth and then living the truth. A lack of endurance is one of the greatest cause of defeat in prayer. Unforgiveness will also hinder our prayers. Prayer is a earthly license for Heavenly interference--GOD works through prayers. Jesus isn't praying for us; He is interceding for us, so we can pray. That is what is meant by asking in His name. (Hebrews 4:16)Let us then approach the throne of grace with confidence so that we may receive mercy and find grace to help us in our time of need. We need to be spiritually sensitive to the fact that GOD is Holy, mighty and worthy to be reverenced. (John 14:15) If you love me, you will obey what I command!! We are cascual about our obedience to GOD. We commit sin and then hurriedly ask for forgiveness. We treat the precious blood of JESUS, which he gave His life to deliver us, as if it's some temporary covering for our messes so we can sin all over again. Sadly, we don't really love JESUS! We use Him. Then we wonder why GOD doesn't answer our prayers. GOD doesn't want us to use Him merely as safety insurance from Hell. He wants a relationship not a religion. TEN STEPS TO PREPAREDNESS IN PRAYER 1.

APPROPRIATE GOD'S GRACE--- He tells us to repent of sin. 2. PUT ON RIGHTEOUSNESS 3. PUT ON TRUTH AND HONESTY 4. CLEANSE WITH THE WORD OF GOD 5. WORSHIP AND PRAISE GOD 6. SEPARATE YOURSELF---If you're going to seek GOD you have to be serious about It. You can't be around distractions. 7. BELIEVE 8. GIVE GOD THE GLORY 9. WASH IN THE WORD 10. REMAIN IN THE RIGHT RELATIONSHIP WITH GOD. POSSIBILITY FAITH MAN'S IMPOSSIBILITY IS GOD'S POSSIBILITY Proverbs 3:5 tells lean not to your own understanding. Get your confession lined up with the word of GOD and exercise your possibility faith. 3 Categories of faith people---1. Excited faith-- they never recognize true facts. 2. Undecided People--they make faith confessions but don't Follow through 3.Positive confession--their armed with greater facts despite the Circumstances. Are you ready to receive what you want? Confess the word of GOD. The word of GOD say: "By His stripes I am healed", "According to His riches in glory all my needs are met", "Greater is he in me than any habit or than any financial difficulty", he's greater than any thing that I can name, "I am more than a conqueror in Christ Jesus". (Mark 11:22-24) What things so ever ye desire when ye pray believe that ye receive them and ye shall have them. Impossibilities can become possibilities if you have the GOD kind of faith. If you're not making your confession based upon the Word of GOD and believing it in your heart you will never get a thing. Don't make confessions out of your head but out of your heart. Keep feeding on the Word and listen to faith testimonies. Hear the Word and your faith will grow. Feed on the Word so you can make the right confessions. Don't claim the devils sickness, pain or poverty. People need the word of GOD so that their faith will come up to the level to receive. Our faith is not in what man can do. Our faith is in what GOD can do. Are you imprisoned by impossibilities. The key to unlock your prison cell is to simply quote the Word of GOD. Take your spiritual vitamins--the Word of GOD--to keep your faith strong. You must keep yourself full of faith. Faith worketh by Love. Because people do not know the Word of GOD, the devil holds them in the prison of impossibilities. Go get the scriptures that has to deal with your particular need or your particular situation and begin to say the Word. You have possibility faith so USE IT!! You're going to have to quote the Word in the face of that impossible situation to make it a possible one. When you're facing temptation, you should be ready--full of what the Word of GOD says and overcome that impossibility by using that Word. If you begin to believe GOD for an impossibility and it doesn't work, your not believing with your heart. Possibility faith is not feelings. It is the Word of GOD. Faith based on feelings come out of your head and you'll be defeated. Natural human faith doesn't work in the spiritual realm because it is of the physical natural body realm and that is where it works. The kind of faith that works in the spirit realm is the GOD kind of faith. Become established in the Word. Make continual statements with possibility faith then and only then will you get results. Then you will walk and live the victorious life, with no defeats. If you mix natural faith and spiritual faith you will have peaks of joy, happiness and victory and you will bottom out in the valley of despair. By using possibility faith you don't have to live like that. No matter what comes you can walk right over the top of every situation. Not because you are superhuman, but because the Word of GOD says so. All things are possible to him that believeth. The more you exercise faith the more it grows. Continue to Thank GOD and keep on quoting the Word, over and over. SAY IT, DO IT, BELIEVE IT AND RECEIVE IT. Are you walking down Victory Boulevard or Defeat Street it's up to you. Know you're a child of GOD and that he loves you no matter what. Learn that He does not cause or allow bad things to happen to you. Your choices in life of your own free will is your own choosing. Don't blame others for your choices. Especially GOD. Know Satan and demons are real. Their job is to steal, kill and destroy. Christians are their #1 target. They're the problem in your life. They want you miserable and in fear. Replace fear with faith. They are very good at their job. They have been working against humanity for over 6000 years. They tell half truths, twisted truths and down right lies. They hate humans for we have a chance at forgiveness and they don't. They can plant the seed of thought but they can't make you do them. You have the choice to act upon these thoughts. So the blame is on you not any one else. Learn you have free will and choice. You're in charge of your own destiny. Your life is based on your own choices. Don't blame GOD. Learn to control your own destiny. The tongue has the power of life or death. Be careful of the words you speak. Never speak negatively. Speak unseen things you want into your life. For example if your child is bad, say over and over how nice and sweet they are. Set an example for others. GOD says you have not because you ask not or you ask for out of Gods' will. Try making a list of things you want in your life. Speak them into existence. Be careful of things you wish for. You also need to be specific. Don't speak bad things into your life by speaking negatively. For example, don't talk about how bad you feel or how broke you are. Remember you are what comes out of your mouth. Always remember the power of your tongue. Never worry about things. Always allow GOD to handle your worries and problems. Give them all to him and know he will handle them. All things are possible with GOD. GOD loves to deal with small problems as well as big ones. He wants you to depend on and trust Him. He loves to do things for his children, if they allow him to. Stop putting yourself first. Don't let Satan tell you that's such a small problem why bother

GOD with it. Can't you do it on your own. Well, maybe you could but our Father enjoys helping us and we can enjoy making Him happy. Tell Satan to back off in JESUS name. If we put GOD first he will take care of everything else. He will provide our needs and if we delight ourselves in him, he will also give us our hearts desires. Surround yourself with positive things. Remember what goes in, will come out. Always give GOD the honor, thanks and glory for all things. Petition GOD for your needs. Allow him to control and lead. Ask for strength and guidance. Never pray for patience, for if you do you will receive trails and tribulations to teach patience to you. Listen to uplifting music, TV and friends. Look for the good in situations not the bad. Remember GOD takes what Satan has meant for evil and makes something good out of it. Learn the power you have as a child of GOD. Always give GOD the credit, for you are nothing without the name of JESUS. Always replace fear with faith. Build your faith daily with the word of GOD. People are influenced by things they see more than things they're told. Let your actions as a child of GOD shine. You can touch others by letting your light shine. If you have a problem give it to GOD and tell him to handle it for you. Praise brings down blessings. Never be ashamed to thank GOD for the things you receive. GOD gives us the power to get wealth. There is power in the blood of JESUS. More power than Satan, demons or any bad situation. So know this and always stand firm on Gods' word. Satan will always lie to you and try to convince you differently. But once you realize God's truth and power the sky's the limit. Every Christian has a divine destiny. We, not GOD, hold the key to our own destiny and future. GOD's direction leads to your divine destiny. It's by faith and patience that we inherit the promises of GOD. Quit trying to put your plan into action. Put His plan into action and receive His best for your life. You will never fulfill your divine destiny if you let your natural man and senses make your decisions and choose your directions. Now, awaken to your divine destiny, go out and represent him and enforce what you've learned. ALL IN THE NAME OF JESUS!!

HELPFUL PRAYERS AND MORE INFORMATION

SIMPLE PRAYER FOR SALVATION

If you don't know Jesus as your personal Lord and Savior, I would like to give you a simple prayer to ask Him into your life. As you say these words out loud, and believe them in your heart. You'll be born again. If you pray this prayer, congratulations you will become a child of GOD. You will be a new creature in Christ Jesus. You will become a citizen of the Kingdom of GOD.

Jesus, come into my life. Forgive me of all my sins, transgressions, and inequities. I ask You to cleanse my heart, and make me a new person in You right now. I believe that You are the Son of GOD and You died on the cross and rose again for me. Jesus, I want to thank You for loving me enough to die for me. I accept all that Your shed blood bought for me

on the cross, and I receive You as my Savior and Lord. Lead me and guide me in your truth. In Jesus Name I Pray. Amen

OUR DAILY PRAYER

Gracious Heavenly Father,

We come to you today to thank you for everything you have done, are doing and will do for us. We thank you for never giving up on us but for redeeming us for yourself and your purposes through your Son, Jesus Christ. Forgive us for being careless and unthinking in the way we approach you. We receive the cleansing of our sins through the blood of Jesus. We worship you in humility and love. Thank you for the privilege of being able to enter with confidence into the place where you dwell because of the atonement that your Son has made on our behalf. We pray that we will not give into the influence and customs of the world around us, but that we will always honor you. Now, let us be your hands and feet. Lead us and guide us

in your truth. Do not let our enemy lead us into the captivity of sin and disobedience. Forgive us for our sins, transgressions, and iniquities. We plead the blood of protection over all of us, our families, friends and loved ones. We rebuke and bind all curses spoken upon us, about us, and by us. I loosen joy, peace and happiness upon all of us. By the authority of the word of GOD, it is written, whatsoever is bound on earth, is bound in heaven, what is loosed on earth, is loosed in Heaven. We stand on the word of GOD and in the name of Jesus Christ our Lord and Savior. Thank you Father for hearing our prayer.

PRAYER FOR YOUR LOVED ONES

Gracious Heavenly Father,

As your child I come to you in petition for my loved one _________(specific name). Thank you Father for hearing and answering my prayer. In Jesus Name. Father lift the veil from _________ that they may see your truth. Open the eyes of their heart and allow the Holy Spirit to hover over _________ and protect them. In Jesus Name. Father cast down anything that would exalt itself against the knowledge of GOD, specifically pride, rebellion, the spirit of addiction, lust and pornography. In Jesus Name. Father take down all known strongholds, thought patterns, opinions on religion, materialism and fear. Father bind Satan and all evil from taking ________ captive, bind all wicked thoughts and lies the enemy tries to place in ______ mind. In Jesus Name. Father rebuke and bind Satan and all evil from the hindrance of _____ hearing and seeing GOD's will and purpose for their life. Loosen GOD'S will , purpose, word and spirit in their life. Father place the armor of GOD on ________ and protect them. Father we ask the you send labors across ______ path daily. Father I plead the blood over ________. In Jesus Name Thank you for all my blessings.

A PRAYER OF DELIVERANCE

IN THE NAME OF THE LORD JESUS CHRIST, and by the power of His blood and the Holy Spirit, I lift to the Lord all of whom I am praying for. Standing on the Word of GOD, I bind all satanic powers, and all evil spirits, occult spirits, spirits of sin, spirits of trauma, familiar spirits, demonic forces, principalities, attributes, aspects, clusters, endowments, satanic thrones, all kings and princes of terrors, and all demonic assignments and functions of destruction from any of these demonic entities of outer space, the air, water, fire, the ground, the netherworld, and evil forces of nature. I bind all interplay, interaction, communication, and all their games between satanic and demonic spirits, out of and away from each and everyone's spirit, soul, mind and body for whom I am praying.

In the name of Jesus. I declare all of you demonic spirits and forces as weakened, defeated enemies of Jesus Christ. I sever all demonic spirits from any demonic ruler above these demonic spirits. I revoke any orders given to any of these demonic spirits and forces as it relates to the lives of all for whom I am praying. I rebuke all spells, hexes, curses, voodoo practices, witchcraft, occult, Masonic and satanic rituals, occult, Masonic and satanic blood covenants, occult, Masonic and satanic blood sacrifices, demonic activities, evil wishes, coven rituals, all occult, Islamic, coven fasting prayers(not of the Lord) and curse-like judgments that have been sent our way, and/or have been passed down through the generational bloodline. I command that they go back to where they came from and be replaced with a blessing. I command that you leave these peoples lives and go straight to the feet of JESUS CHRIST NOW! I ask forgiveness for and renounce, all negative inner vows made by myself and by those for whom I am praying. Their assignments and influences in the lives of those people and areas are broken. In the name of JESUS. I ask that Jesus Christ release us from any vows and from bondage they may have held in us. Thank you Lord that you will not remember the iniquities of our forefathers against us. By the power of GOD'S Holy Word, I take the sword of the spirit and cut every person free from all generational inherited sin, weaknesses, character defects, personality traits, cellular disorders, genetic disorders, learned negative inner vows, spiritual and psychological ties. I cut all bonds that are not of the Lord and put His cross between us, our parents, our grandparents, our siblings, our offspring, our mates(and any relationships that our mates have had with others in the past). I cut all bonds of the relationships of each one of us that are not of the Lord back to the beginning of time, by the sword of the spirit, by the Word of GOD, and in the name of JESUS, I say that we are cut free and we are free indeed. We are now free to become the children of God the Lord intended us to be. I ask that GOD send the Holy Spirit, and the holy angels of GOD to surround and protect each area and individual and to seek out and cleanse with GOD's holy light all areas vacated by the forces of evil. I ask the Holy Spirit to permeate our spirits, minds, souls, and bodies, creating a hunger and thirst for GOD's Holy Word and to fill us to overflowing with the life and love of JESUS CHRIST and His Holy Spirit. Lord awaken our sleeping spirits and bring us into the light. Transform us by the renewing of our minds daily in Christ Jesus. Pour out your spirit on us, reveal your Word to us, give your angels charge over us in all our ways. Thank you Lord for everything. In the name of Jesus.

"AND THE GATES OF HELL SHALL NOT PREVAIL AGAINST IT" WHATSOEVER THOU SHALT BIND ON EARTH SHALL BE BOUND IN HEAVEN: AND WHATSOEVER THOU SHALT LOOSE ON EARTH SHALL BE LOOSEN IN HEAVEN(Matt. 16:18,19) THIS PRAYER IS THE FIRST STEP TO HEALING (Prayer should be out loud)

Lord Jesus Christ, I believe you died on the cross for my sins and rose again from the dead. You redeemed my by your blood and I belong to you, and I want to live for you. I confess all my sins---known and unknown---I'm sorry for them all. I renounce them all. I forgive all others, as I want you to forgive me. Forgive me now and cleanses me with your blood. I thank you for the blood of JESUS CHRIST which cleanses me now from my special needs---the thing that binds, that torments, that defiles; that evil spirit, that unclean spirit---I claim the promise of your word, "Whosoever that calleth on the name of the Lord shall be delivered." I call upon you now. In the name of the LORD JESUS CHRIST, deliver me and set me free. Satan, I renounce you and all your works. I loose myself from you, in the name of

JESUS, and I command you to leave me right now, in JESUS name. Amen!! Our Father, who art rich in mercy and compassion. I pray Thou would hear the utterances of my soul. O Thou Redeemer, be my strength in the flood, and let my trust always rest in Thee. Let my soul feel thy pardoning grace that I might be restored to favor with thee. Let Thy glory appear, that we might find peace for the coming and closing of each day. May we rejoice over Thy marvelous works. Now, Lord I rebuke and bind the spirit of infirmities from my body and the damage that they have caused in the name of JESUS. I cast out(your specific sickness and disease and the damage that they cause). I am a child of GOD and I know my rights. You are a trespasser and you must go. I command you to go now in the name of JESUS. For by His stripes we were healed. JESUS bored our sickness and disease. I tell you that you have no right to stay in my body for I belong to JESUS CHRIST. JESUS purchased me with His own blood. You are a trespasser and you must go. I command you to go now in the name of JESUS. Preserve me, O GOD: for in thee do I put my trust. Let the words of my mouth, and the meditation of my heart, be acceptable in Thy sight O Lord, my strength, and my Redeemer. In Jesus Name Amen. Lord baptize me with the HOLY SPIRIT. Lord loosen the fruits of the spirit upon me, Love, Joy, Peace, Longsuffering, Gentleness, Faith, Meekness, and Temperance. Fill me with your Holy Spirit in Jesus Name. Thank you Gracious Heavenly Father for all you have done, all you are doing, and all you are going to do. With joy we praise Thy name forever and ever, through Christ Jesus our Lord. Praise you Lord and Thank you Jesus.

ALL THE LAW AND THE PROPHETS HANG ON THESE TWO COMMANDMENTS. LOVE THE LORD YOUR GOD WITH ALL YOUR HEART AND WITH ALL YOUR SOUL AND WITH ALL YOUR MIND! THIS IS THE FIRST AND GREATEST COMMANDMENT. AND THE SECOND ONE IS LIKE IT: LOVE YOUR NEIGHBOR AS YOURSELF. Put these two first and these ten will follow! THOU SHALT HAVE NO OTHER GODS BEFORE ME---THOU SHALT NOT MAKE ANY GRAVEN IMAGE---THOU SHALT NOT TAKE THE NAME OF THE LORD THY GOD IN VAIN---REMEMBER THE SABBATH DAY, TO KEEP IT HOLY---HONOR THY FATHER AND MOTHER---THOU SHALT NOT KILL---THOU SHALT NOT COMMIT ADULTERY---THOU SHALT NOT STEAL---THOU SHALT NOT BEAR FALSE WITNESS AGAINST THY NEIGHBOR---THOU SHALT NOT COVET.

MARRIAGE TAKES THREE

Marriage takes three to be complete---It's not enough for two to meet---They must be united in love---By love's creator, GOD above---Then their love will be firm and strong---Able to last when things go wrong---Because they've felt GOD's love and know---He's always there, He'll never go---And they have both loved Him in kind---With all the heart and soul and mind---And in that love they've found the way---To love each other every day---A marriage that follows GOD's plan---Takes more than a woman and a man---It needs a oneness that can be--------------Only from CHRIST-----------Marriage takes three------------

THE IMPORTANCE AND DANGERS OF THE LORD'S SUPPER OR THE COMMUNION OF THE BLOOD OF

-----------------------CHRIST----------------------

The Lord's supper is in representation of the suffering and beating of Christ's body and the shedding of blood for our sins. The bread was broken, symbolizing the marred and striped body of Christ, for our healing. He bore our sickness and our diseases. Thus by His stripes we were healed.(I Peter 2:24) As a child of GOD this is our right and promise, but we must claim it. The juice symbolizes the blood of Christ, shed for the remission of sins. It represents the blood covenant with Christ and the believers. This entitles Children of GOD all of GOD'S promises, but again we must claim them. It is also the blessing cup. It is a remembrance of the death of Christ until he comes again. It will be observed by Christ and all believers in the Kingdom of GOD forever. It is not to be partaken unworthly. It should be partaken in faith and proper examination of self or condemnation, sickness, and even death may result. It should not be taken by an unsaved man with sin in the life and without making proper confession and acknowledgement of Christ as Lord and Savior. It should not be taken without judging oneself so as to escape chastening from GOD. Before partaking one should carefully examine ones, life confess any sins, and ask for forgiveness. It should not be taken to commemorate a mere historical fact or just as a tradition. It should not be taken in unbelief, not realizing it's true significance, not discerning the Lord's body and blood to receive the benefits by faith.(I Cor 18-32)

GOD'S NUMBER SYSTEM FOR SUCCESS

7 IS GOD'S NUMBER FOR COMPLETION
10 IS GOD'S NUMBER FOR PERFECTION
ZERO(0) TO OUR FLESH IS OUR GOAL
TO BE 100% SPIRIT FILLED
YOU CAN NOT BE FULL OF THE SPIRIT AND WALKING IN HIS WAYS IF YOUR FULL OF YOURSELF

GOD'S FORMULA FOR REACHING THIS GOAL
Please follow instructions carefully

FOR 7 DAYS A WEEK PUT GOD'S WORDS IN YOUR HEART ONCE YOU HAVE BECOME A 10, YOU WILL BE A ZERO(0) TO YOUR FLESH WHICH WILL GIVE YOU 100% SPIRIT FILLED LIFE. THIS WILL GIVE YOU THE MORE ABUNDANT LIFE PROMISED US IN JOHN 10:10 "BELOVED, I WISH ABOVE ALL THINGS THAT THOU MAYEST PROSPER AND BE IN HEALTH, EVEN AS THY SOUL PROSPERETH." III JOHN 2

"WHATSOEVER A MAN SOWETH THAT SHALL HE ALSO REAP" GALATIONS 6:7

SOW GOD'S FORMULA FOR SUCCESS AND WATCH HIS PROMISES APPEAR!!

POEMS BY CLAUDIA
BEWARE HUMAN BEWARE

Promises made, not to your surprise
soon to be forgotten
with lingering words and uncontrollable thoughts
love turns to hate and seals your fate
as time passes on, dreams shatter like glass
twisted smiles cover the truth
the war rages on from the beginning of time
you're a prisoner of your humanity

BEWARE HUMAN BEWARE
Searching for the light with pain as black as night
Dreams tearing at your soul as darkness creeps in
Blinded of the TRUTH, underneath it all
Sending perilous tides from the other side
Only victims of his deception

Locked in fear, emerged in selfishness
drenched in your pride, engulfed by distrust
kills the last chance of hope
while passing trends fuel spiritual hunger

and emptiness prevails
Nowhere to run,
Nowhere to hide
behind it all, the master of lies
fallen from heaven
blameless in his ways until unrighteous set in
the father of lies and "I WILLS
BEWARE HUMAN BEWARE

SOLDIER

The war that we fight--- is not flesh and blood
with this in mind--- stay alert--- keep praying
the one in me is greater than he
so why don't you take up the spirit--- LET'S FIGHT

If you hear His voice--- don't harden your heart
put on your armor--- stand strong in TRUTH
washed in the Blood--- shielded by Faith
COME BE A SOLDIER WITH ME

The Word of GOD is a double-edged sword
be merciful to those that doubt
snare others from the fire
stand your ground--- stand firm in Love
put GOD's Word in your mouth
bring forth an overflow of glory
COME BE A SOLDIER
COME BE A SOLDIER FOR GOD

PACK YOUR BAGS

Are you sick
Do you ache with pain
Are you a child of GOD
Do you think that you're just human
And that's just part of life
WELL! NEWS FLASH
If you're a child of GOD
Walking the walk and talking the talk
quit swallowing Satan's lies!!!
For I'm a faith walkin', bible totin', scripture quotin', spirit-taught, wide-eyed, sanctified, blood-bought, child of GOD that loves Satan bashing and sin trashin'
So! Satan pack your bags
you're not welcome here no more
cause Christ moved in
and kicked you out the door
Satan pack your bags you're not welcome here no more

It's time you learned the TRUTH

You're not just human
break the chains of humanity and step over into the light
If you'll stop walkin' in the flesh and start walkin' in the spirit--- You'll know by His stripes you were already healed
Satan doesn't have the right to make you sick

WOKE FROM A DREAM

I woke from a dream
and wiped the sweat from my brow
it didn't seem possible
I didn't know how

I was always a good person
and knew JESUS was the way
but life's everyday business had led me astray
I had listened to the whisper's
Telling put myself first
And when you pray your life only gets worse

The lies kept repeating
And then finally I believed
Falling in the rut of being one deceived
Things I never dreamed of doing was an everyday affair
Things would seem so bad at times
I felt like pullin' out my hair

But in the darkness in my sleep

Someone was callin' me
He said dear child just turn around
And I will set you free

I didn't want to hear it and I pushed the thoughts aside
The life that I was living was a totally big lie
Never thinking about mercy or the reason for this state
the path that I was walking was only sealin' up my fate

I wanted to believe that I was happy with my life
in my dazed confusion thought partying' was the life
the rough crowd that I was hangin' with
knew not to make me mad
see I had a reputation to keep and it was really bad
but now looking back on that life it is really very sad
to think of the years I had lost and of the very cost now

thankful for the waking dream and
the call to glory bound
if you're in this state of mind I hope

that you will find that JESUS is the answer and he will set you free for happiness is being blessed then you will surely see that life is more than just being ME-ME-ME

RAT RACE

Living in the so called rat race
day after day
sunrise to midnight
running to and fro
step back look at your life
for this world in it's present form
is passing away
what's important to you
your job
your possessions
your free time
where does GOD fall on your list
remember a man reaps what he sows

JESUS return is near
sand in the hour glass is low
like a thief in the night
the lightening will flash
the thunder will roll

America once beautiful
walkin' in His ways
fallen from grace
turn away your evil ways
far from the roots of GOD
having a form of Godliness
but denying His power
I pray that the eyes of your hearts be enlightened
instead of earthly things
set your minds on things above

Jesus return is near
Sand in the hour glass is low- like a thief in the night
The lightning will flash
The thunder will roll
for the trumpets will blow
the dead will arise
in the twinkle of an eye
we'll be called up high
two will be standing
one will be taken
the other one left
which will you be
how important will your list be
on the day of JESUS return
WAKE UP
SPEAK THE TRUTH OF LOVE!!!!!!!!!!!

SUPERMAN

GOD is my Superman
all we have to do is follow His plan
His kryptonite is our disbelief
that causes so much sorrow and grief

in the beginning He created the heavens and earth
and made man from the dirt
then man fell like Satan from grace
and GOD had to turn away His face

GOD told his people just believe
Noah built the ark--- you know the history
he called upon Moses--- to part the Red Sea
David slay a giant with just a little stone
Daniel slept with the lions---there is no mystery

He sent His only begotten Son
He healed the lame and made the blind man see
He said dear children come and follow me
He stretched out His hand to Peter on the water

He stretched out His hands for Thomas to see
He stretched out His hand for you and me
JESUS IS MY SUPERMAN
All we have to do is follow His plan
His kryptonite is our disbelief
that causes so much sorrow and grief
He came to earth and hung on a tree
He came to earth to set man free
He wants to show us the way
All we have to do is trust and obey
put away your kryptonite turn your darkness into light
and go with Him on that heavenly flight
JESUS IS OUR SUPERMAN

JUNE 2001

NOTHING MAN

Using worldly wisdom
you think you're all so smart
ice water flows through your veins
to a frozen mass
you call a heart
the blackness inside
over shadows all the pain
working for yourself
in the end
will bring no gain
never thinking about nothing
on the climb to the top
others feelings
crushed all the way
beneath the cold hard rock

everything you do
everything you say
nothing but yourself
is the business of your day

you're a nothing man
with the world
as your temptress
and yourself as your god
you're a nothing man
everyday you need a worldly fix
a social drink
a smoke or toke
just to make it through the day
a pill to wake
a pill to sleep
and don't forget to play
blending up a deadly mix
in the name of fun
life in the fast lane
always keeps you on the run---

no mercy
no love
don't get in my way
I'm the boss
I run my life
isn't that what you always say
the interest will be great
the awesome price you'll pay

the ultimate cost
will be your loss
at the end of life's highway
come and let me whisper
the error of you way
everything you do
everything you say
nothing but yourself
is the business of your day
with the world as your temptress
and yourself as your god
you're a nothing man
KING NOTHING

MORE MAJOR ATTACKS FROM THE ENEMY

GOD will take what is meant for evil and make good for those who love him and follow His ways. He never said there would not be times in the pit but the time spent in the pit will depend on how your handled the situations. Your way or by GOD's word.---Oct. 97--I moved Alice(Jeff's mom) in with us. She could no longer live alone; she had Huntington's disease. It took 6 months but Miss Alice accepted Jesus as Lord and Savior.---Dawn (my daughter) went to ER. She had a large cystic on her ovary causing severe bleeding. We prayed then at her Dr. appointment 3 days later they could not find a cystic.--- June 97 Miss Alice pulled her feeding tube out. We went to the ER. Where her feeding tube was replaced wrong and she almost died. She went through emergency surgery, was in ICU for 10 days, and a nursing home for 8 months. She recovered from 65lbs., bedridden in a diaper to 95lbs. And walking again. I brought her back home for another 2 ½ yrs, before she had to go back to a nursing home.---Uncle Yank died of a massive heart attack.---Papa Hobbs died of strokes in Dec. 98.---Both my sons wreaked twice but were O.K.---Breaker box on the outside of my house caught fire and only smoked the shingles around it.---Melba (my ex-mother-in-law) died but she accepted Jesus with me during her battle with cancer.---Dawn wrecked after taking the neighborhood kids to Super Saturday at our church. Paramedics said she had a concussion and needed stitches in her arm but she was ok when we got to the ER. Her head hit the windshield so hard that her hair was left in it. It was a freak accident just out of the neighbor's driveway. The neighbor was driving and her arm was broken in several places.---Chevy (Melba's grandson) died in a car wreck at 16, one mile from his home.---Uncle Joe (Melba's son) in which Chevy was living with, wanted to commit suicide when told of Chevy's death. I went to ER. And rebuked that spirit from him.---Two months later Chris(Chevy's mother) was killed in a work accident.---May 2000, my house caught on fire from electrical. Shawn (my son) caught it before it was too bad. The house needed lots of repair, so Jeff quit his good job to get his 401k to go with the insurance money and we totally remodeled. The fireman that was doing the report for us, father had a heart attack, wrecked and died instantly which held up our insurance. Jeff got a job as soon as we finished remodeling the house. The first day he went to put in applications, after returning home, there was a message from an old co-worker asking if he wanted to come work for him. This man did not know Jeff was looking for work

My dad's car was stolen and recovered later. I had put the thief in the Lord's hands. Two weeks later the thief was stabbed to death over a drug deal at the crack house where he had sold the car parts.---Shane (my son) was rushed to the ER. With kidney stones. I arrived and we prayed. They told him no surgery but he should pass it in several days. He never hurt again and he never passed the large stone that was shone on the test.---Dec. 28, 2000 my grandmother was a victim of our areas only home invasion. She was left for dead but she awoke in a pool of blood at 6a.m. and called my mom. I was awakened at 3:30a.m. and I couldn't breath. I started praying even though I didn't know why, but this was the time the intruder was smothering her. When we arrived at the ER. She was beaten very badly and she was 84. She recovered and was very blessed to survive.---My mom fell and broke her arm.---Kim(a friend) wrecked with her mom and two small children. Her mom died instantly. Kim and two children recovered. The people who hit them left them in a burning car to die but the Lord had other plans. Kim's mom had accepted Jesus two days earlier at my home. Kim accepted Jesus in her hospital room.---My house burned again in Aug. 2002. We had just refinanced and made our first payment. It was gutted this time but GOD makes good out of evil so we rearranged walls and have a brand new home now.---Uncle Odell died of a massive heart attack.---An older lady hit our blazer on the driver's side. All new parts were used and it was fixed like new.---I was offered a voluntary chaplain position at a new Hospice Center, by Rev. R.D. Woods, the man who remodeled our home. Rev. Woods ordained me where I could take the *position. This cause a major attack from the enemy and I almost lost everything, my husband, family, home, everything the Lord had blessed me with. But the Lord stepped in and stopped that. The job was given to someone else because funding became available to pay someone.---I hit a pole at Captain D's drive-thru but they helped pay the deductible.---Aunt Cecil died.---A casserole dish exploded on the stove with Devin and me next to it. Glass was everywhere except on Devin and me. ---A friend's small son was diagnosed with M.D.---An $8000 nursing home bill for Alice, hung over my head. Medicaid later paid it after a year of praying. They say Medicaid never changes their minds, but all things are possible with GOD.---Oct. 26, 2004 Crystal's(Shane's girlfriend) mom died at the age of 54, in her sleep.---The night of November 10, 2004 started a major attack that seemed like would never end. I received a phone call after midnight Nov. 11. My son (Shane) had been in a truck wreck. He had been in an argument with Crystal; he was alone, angry and driving to fast. He lost control of his small pick up, rolled three times and was thrown 100ft. GOD was there for him that night. A policeman saw the accident and had an ambulance* *there immediately. He was air lifted to UAB. Later I was told of the awesome presence of GOD on the scene. God took good care of Shane for me. They said it was like he was wearing an invisible helmet. He had no head trauma or spinal injuries. Even though the trauma flight paramedic picked six pounds of glass from his face, he had not one scratch to his eyes or any broken teeth. He did have a broken collar bone, torn artery in his left arm, seven brakes in his right arm, broken pelvic bone and lots of road rash. I can't go into all the details for the would take a whole book but they said his recovery would take 6 months to a year. We went home after 5 weeks in TBICU and he was walking in three months. While I was with Shane at UAB, Satan attacked Devin(my 3yr.old grandson) Devin began having headaches that became severe. Dawn (my daughter)did not tell me that Devin was that sick. She felt that I was burdened enough dealing with Shane's accident. She took him to several Dr.'s and two different ER's several times. It was always the same, he's ok, and he's just having sinus problems. Then it was his adenoids, which they removed the week before Shane came home from UAB (Dec. 15th). On Dec. 17th at 10:30 p.m.,*

Dawn called, Devin was non responsive and the paramedics were on their way. I was there before them and when they arrived the ambulance rushed Devin to the ER. He was awake by then but screaming with his head hurting. Dawn had begged them to do a CT several times before, but they would not. That night it was done immediately. Results showed a large brain tumor attached to the base of his brain stem. He was rushed to Children's Hospital. Before surgery I was able to pray with Devin. After surgery the tumor was removed, it was not attached to anything and it was the size of a grape. They said they didn't know how that he had endured the pain from the excessive fluid built up on his brain. The worst was that he had cancer cells in the lining of his brain. Jan. 2nd, at 1a.m. they said that he wouldn't make it till 7:30a.m. I prayed and stood on psalms 91 and he was stable at 7:00a.m. He went through several months of painful chemo and lots of tests. We watched miracle after miracle then all of a sudden the cancer returned worse than before. They had been in the hospital for five months. Dawn chose to stop the chemo and spend the remaining time with him at home. April 23rd magic moments, sent us to Gulf Shores for Devin to see the beach. He did better that week than the whole five months in the hospital. The week before this began he told his dad that he was going to be a fisherman of men. He knew Jesus very well despite his age. Devin has touch lots of people during his courageous battle with cancer and he is still touching others through his testimony. Devin was and is a fisherman of men. Devin went home to be with Jesus May 7th 2005. That was the hardest thing I have ever endured. But I will praise the Lord even in the storm

My grandmother had a stroke, fell and broke her hip.---June 5th my dad had a light heart attack. They said he needed heart surgery but they could not do it because of his lungs.---June 23rd Shane had wrist surgery on his right arm. They removed three small bones to relieve the pain and give it more movement. He no longer has strength in that hand.---July 19th Crystal hurt Shane's hand during an argument. Had to take him to St. Vincent's for x-rays.---July 25th Crystal came with a positive pregnancy test.---July 27th Shane had surgery on wrist to remove pins.---Masie Knight (a friend) lost her battle with cancer.---Sept. 15th Alice (Jeff's mom) died in the nursing home---Sept. 22nd John

Peoples (a cousin) on death row was executed.---I stopped keeping track of things after that.---Since then My dad died Dec. 22nd, 2006. Grandpa Charlie died and Jeff's brother was killed at 17 in a car accident. Now my major battle is with a horrible disease that Jeff has inherited from his mom. Huntington's Disease is a rare inherited disease that is all the bad things rolled into one. It kills parts of your brain. There is no treatment or cure. These are just some of the major battles fought, but still I'm going strong for my Lord Jesus Christ. I don't know how people make it without him. See once you become a threat to the enemy you become his target. Being a Christian is not easy, some people even see Christians as weak and wimpy. The truth is that it is much easier to do just as you please with no respect for yourself or others. Selfishness is the major human downfall. The I, I, I, or me, me, me, syndrome. The fact is we must respect and care for our fellowman which is hard to do without the love of Christ in our hearts. When we began to serve the Lord, we become a threat to Satan. We must learn GOD's plan of protection. Even then Satan will throw attacks but we have the authority in Jesus Name to protect us. Attacks are strategies. What he fears the most is what he attacks the most. The area of your attacks are a revelations of what the enemy fears the most about you. We are told to fight the good fight, for we are in a spiritual war. The fight is for souls not to go to hell. We must care enough to save our fellowman and share the good news of salvation. The more of a threat the stronger the attacks. I will continue my fight for the Lord Jesus Christ because each soul is precious and eternity is forever.

GOD'S WORD ON THE LAST DAYS

You will hear of wars and rumors of wars, but see to it that your are not alarmed. Such things must happen, but the end is still to come. Nation will rise against nation, and kingdom against kingdom. There will be famines and earthquakes in various places. All these are the beginning of birthing pains. Like a woman in labor, the pains, like events become stronger and closer together. You will be handed over to be persecuted and put to death, and you will be hated by all nations because of me. At that time many will turn away from the faith and will betray and hate each other and many false prophets will appear and deceive many people. In latter times, some will abandon the faith and follow deceiving spirits and things taught by demons. Not only do they become idlers, but also gossips and busybodies, saying things they ought not to. Some have in fact already turned away to follow Satan. Because of the increase of wickedness, the love of most will grow cold, but he who stands firm to the end will be saved. And this gospel of the kingdom will be preached in the whole world as a testimony to all nations, and then the end will come. So when you see standing in the Holy place the abomination that causes desolation, look up for your redemption is near. For then there will be great distress, unequaled from the beginning of the world until now---and never to be equaled again. Immediately after the distress of those days "the sun will be darkened and the moon will not give its light; the stars will fall from the sky, and the heavenly bodies will be shaken." At that time the sign of the Son of Man will appear in the sky, and all the nations of the earth will mourn. They will see the Son of Man coming on the clouds of the sky, with power and great glory. And he will send his angels with a loud trumpet call, and they will gather his elect from the four winds, from one end of the heavens to the other. When you see all these things, you will know that it is near, right at the door. I tell you the TRUTH, this generation will certainly not pass away until all these things have been. No one knows about that day or hour, not even the angels in heaven, not the Son, but only the Father. It will be as in the days of Noah, before the flood. People were eating, drinking, partying, doing their own thing and they knew nothing about what would happen until the flood came and took them all away. That is how it is today. Therefore keep watch because you do not know on what day your Lord will come but he did give us the signs of the last days. There will terrible times in the last days. People will be lovers of themselves, lovers of money, boastful, proud, abusive, disobedient to their parent's, ungrateful, unholy, without love, unforgiving, slanderous, without self-control, brutal, not lovers of the good, treacherous, rash, conceited, lovers of pleasure rather than lovers of GOD---having a form of godliness but denying its power. They are the kind who worm their way into homes and gain control over the weak-willed, who are loaded down with sins and are swayed by all kinds of evil desires, always learning but never able to acknowledge the TRUTH. For it will come upon all those who live on the face of the whole earth. Be always on the watch and pray that you may be able to escape all that is about to happen and that you may be able to stand before the Son of Man. This generation will certainly not end until all these things have happened. According to the bible, a generation is around 70 years. End time prophecies tells us the beginning of that last generation began with the rebirth of Israel, on May 15, 1948.(Isaiah 66:8, Ezekiel 4:3-6) Israel will be immediately surrounded by enemies.(Psalms 83:2-8) The miraculous restoration of the Hebrew language. (Zeph. 3:9) The return of the Ethiopian Jews to Israel. Both Russia(north) and Ethiopia(south). (Ezekiel 37:21)Foretold of the return of the exiles to the Holy Land. The astonishing fertility of Israel. Isaiah predicted that Israel would become fertile again in Isaiah 27:6. Joel declared that Israel would experience tremendous increases of rain in the last days.(Joel 2:23) Israel's plans to rebuild the temple.(Isaiah 2:2, Rev. 11:1,2). The key ingredients for the oil of anointing were thought to be lost forever were recently found.(Daniel 9:24, Exodus 30:25,26) The vessels for the future temple worship were also found.(Ezekiel 44:16,17--36:25) The revival of the Roman Empire(Daniel 2:40-44,7, Rev. 13,17) The rebuilding of Babylon(Iraq) (Isaiah

34:8-10) The creation of a one world government. (Daniel 7:14, Rev. 13:7,8) The rising power of the United Nations, the World Trade Organization, World Court, and the economic downfalls are moving us quickly beyond the days of national sovereignty and individual nations. For nation shall rise against nation and kingdom against kingdom; and there shall be famines and pestilences and earthquakes in divers places.(Zech.14:12, Matt.24:7) Worldwide famine.(Rev. 6:5) The rise in major "killer" earthquakes told by Jesus--Ezekiel--Zechariah--Haggi-- and John. Preparations with modern technology for the mark of the Beast (Rev. 13:16-18). People around the world will see the two prophets killed is now possible with modern day technology.(Rev. 11:9,10) Gospel of the Kingdom shall be preached in all the World(Matt. 24:14) Knowledge and travel shall increase in the last days(Daniel 12:4) Preparations for the battle of Armageddon are happening now(Rev. 16:16) John also stated the army of the eastern nations would consist of an astonishing two hundred million soldiers. China can now fulfill this.(Rev. 9:15-16) A military highway across Asia and the drying up of the Euphrates River(Rev. 16:12) And as of today

January 2011(Isaiah 19:2) a civil war in Egypt will take place in connection with last day events. Wake up people it's closer than you think! We're living in the last generation that will not end before His return! Wow! What an amazing time in history to live in, to watch prophecy happen right before our very eyes daily.

THE SIGNS OF THE AGES

THE SIGNS OF THE AGES HAS APPEARED
SATAN AND HIS DEMONS TREMBLE IN FEAR
HIS TIME GROWS SHORT NOW YOU SEE
AS PROPHETS OF OLD HAS THUS FORETOLD
HIS LEASE ON EARTH HAS NOW BEEN SOLD
JESUS PAID THE PRICE FOR YOU AND ME
WHEN HE SHED HIS BLOOD ON CALVARY

THE CHOSEN GENERATION BEGAN IN FORTY-EIGHT
WHEN ISRAEL REBORN SEALED SATAN'S FATE
IT CAME INTO EXISTENCE IN JUST ONE DAY
JUST AS ISAIAH PRECISELY SAID
IMMEDIATELY SURROUND BY HER ENEMIES
KING DAVID SAID CHILDREN LIFT UP THY HEADS

SEE THIS GENERATION WILL NOT END

THE STORY'S BEEN WRITTEN AND HIS ANGELS
HE'LL SEND GATHERING HIS CHILDREN OF
THE CHURCH
DON'T BE LOST DURING THAT SEARCH
FOR THE SIGNS OF THE AGES HAS NOW
APPEARED
WITH JESUS AS OUR SAVIOR WE HAVE NO
FEAR
HE PAID THE PRICE FOR YOU AND ME
WHEN HE SHED HIS BLOOD ON CALVARY

JEWS NOW RETURNING BOTH DAY AND NIGHT
WITH NO ONE STOPPING THEM IN THIS
FLIGHT
THE LAND NOW FERTILE LIKE DAYS OF OLD
WITH INCREASES OF RAIN THAT WAS TOLD BY
JOEL
PERSEQUTION, RIDICULE, SON AGAINST
FATHER
LOVERS OF THEMSELVES AND THE ALL
MIGHTY DOLLAR
IT'S ENOUGH TO MAKE A RIGHTEOUS MAN
STAND UP AND HOLLER
IF THAT'S NOT ENOUGH PROOF THEN WHY
SHOULD I BOTHER!!!

HOW TO WIN AS A SUCCESSFUL MATURE CHRISTIAN

USE DAILY SCRIPTURES TO FED ON FOR SUCCESS

Jesus tells us My people perish for lack of knowledge. Just like man's law's claim ignorance of the law does not make you not guilty. Remember Matt. 7, do not judge if you do you will be judged with the measure you use; it will be measured to you. Realize as a child of GOD, he does discipline his children out of love. Read Hebrews 12:7-11; time for discipline yields peaceful fruit, righteousness to those who have been trained by it. When you're already a born again Christian, John 3:16, learn you're a child of GOD. Learn GOD's promises for you as his children and how to stand on them. Please read I and II Timothy. These are helpful on how to act. Know your living a blessing or a curse. Read Deut. 11:26. Deut. 30:15, tells us it's all our choice, "See I set before you today life and prosperity---death and destruction". For GOD's plan for prosperity read Deut. 14:22 "Be sure to set aside a tenth of all that your fields produce each year." GOD's plan for life, sin causes death. Sickness is part of the curses listed in Deut. 28:15. Jesus conquered sickness for His children. Learn this and claim it for it tells us; "By His stripes we were healed. Learn how important the words are that come out of your mouth. Begin to place the following scriptures in your heart where you can stand strong on GOD's Word daily. KEY WORD IS DAILY! ALSO PRAY OUT LOUD! Please turn and read these following scriptures. LUKE 12:30---TELLS US TO SEEK THE KINGDOM FIRST---MATT. 22:37-39---TELLS US THE FIRST AND GREATEST COMMANDMENT---LOVE THE LORD YOUR GOD WITH ALL YOUR HEART, MIND, AND SOUL.---Love is a precious virtue in the kingdom of GOD, the controlling principle of heaven, and the glue that holds everything together. There are three things that will endure-faith, hope, and love-and the greatest of these is love. Let love be your highest goal. Love is patient and kind. Love is not jealous or boastful or proud or rude. Love does not demand its own way. Love is not irritable, and it keeps no record of wrong. It is never glad about injustice but rejoices when the truth wins out. Love never gives up, never loses faith, is always hopeful, and endures through every circumstance. Love is the very nature of GOD. For GOD is love.---EPHESIANS 6:10-18---KNOW WHO YOUR ENEMY IS! FOR OUR STRUGGLE IS NOT FLESH AND BLOOD. LEARN YOUR ARMOR AND HOW TO FIGHT.---JAMES 4:10---HUMBLE YOURSELF BEFORE THE LORD AND HE WILL LIFT YOU UP---I PETER 4:2---DO NOT LIVE THE REST OF YOUR EARTHLY LIFE FOR EVIL HUMAN DESIRES, BUT RATHER FOR THE WILL OF GOD---PSALMS 37:1-4---DO NOT FRET BECAUSE OF EVIL MEN OR BE ENVIOUS OF THOSE WHO DO WRONG; FOR LIKE GRASS THEY WILL SOON WITHER, LIKE GREEN PLANTS THEY WILL SOON DIE AWAY. TRUST IN THE LORD AND DO GOOD, DWELL IN THE LAND AND ENJOY SAFE PASTURE. DELIGHT YOURSELF IN THE LORD AND HE WILL GIVE YOU THE DESIRES OF YOUR HEART---MARK 9:23---EVERYTHING IS POSSIBLE FOR HIM

WHO BELIEVES---II TIM. 2:24---THE LORD'S SERVANT MUST NOT QUARREL; INSTEAD HE MUST BE KIND TO EVERYONE, ABLE TO TEACH, NOT RESENTFUL.---JOHN 14:12---I TELL YOU THE TRUTH ANYONE WHO HAS FAITH IN ME WILL DO WHAT I HAVE BEEN DOING . HE WILL DO EVEN GREATER THINGS THAN THESE.---PROV. 13:3---HE WHO GUARDS HIS LIPS GUARDS HIS LIFE, BUT HE WHO SPEAKS RASHLY WILL COME TO RUIN---PROV. 17:14---STARTING A QUARREL IS LIKE BREACHING A DAM, SO DROP THE MATTER BEFORE A DISPUTE BREAKS OUT.---JAMES 1:19---BE SLOW TO SPEAK AND SLOW TO ANGER.---I PETER 2:17---SHOW PROPER RESPECT TO EVERYONE---PROV. 15:1---A GENTLE ANSWER TURNS AWAY WRATH, BUT A HARSH WORD STIRS UP ANGER---JAMES 5:9---DON'T GRUMBLE AGAINST EACH OTHER---I THESS. 5:14---LIVE IN PEACE WITH EACH OTHER---JAMES 3:16---ENVY AND SELFISH AMBITION FIND DISORDER AND EVIL PRACTICE---LUKE 11:23---HE WHO IS NOT WITH ME IS AGAINST ME---PROV. 18:21---THE TONGUE HAS THE POWER OF LIFE AND DEATH, SO BE CAREFUL

OF THE WORDS OF YOUR MOUTH---PHILP.4:6---DON'T BE ANXIOUS ABOUT ANYTHING---PHILP.4:11-13---I HAVE STRENGHT FOR ALL THINGS IN CHRIST WHO ENPOWERS ME---I PETER 5:7---CAST ANXIETY AND WORRY ON JESUS---COLO 3:17---DO EVERYTHING IN THE NAME OF JESUS---PROV. 28:20---A FAITHFUL MAN WILL BE RICHLY BLESSED---HEBREWS 10:25---DON'T FORSAKE THE MEETING TOGETHER---ACTS 4:29---NOW LORD CONSIDER THEIR THREATS AND ENABLE YOUR SERVANT TO SPEAK YOUR WORD WITH GREAT BOLDNESS---I JOHN 4:4---HE THAT IS IN ME IS GREATER THAN HE THAT IS IN THE WORLD---II THESS. 3:3---THE LORD IS FAITHFUL AND HE WILL STRENGTHEN AND PROTECT YOU FROM THE EVIL ONE---PROV 13:2---FROM THE FRUIT OF HIS LIPS A MAN ENJOYS GOOD THINGS---PSALMS 91:9---IF YOU MAKE THE MOST HIGH YOUR DWELLING EVEN THE LORD WHO IS MY REFUGE-THEN NO HARM WILL BEFALL YOU, NO DISASTER WILL COME NEAR YOUR TENT. FOR HE WILL COMMAND HIS ANGELS CONCERNING YOU, TO GUARD YOU IN ALL YOUR WAYS!---ISAIAH

54:17---NO WEAPON FORGED AGAINST ME SHALL PROSPER---PROV 13:22---A GOOD MAN LEAVES AN INHERITANCE FOR HIS CHILDREN'S CHILDREN, BUT A SINNERS WEALTH IS STORED UP FOR THE RIGHTEOUS---USE GOD'S COMMAND IN TIME'S OF TROUBLE. SAY OUT LOUD: LORD REBUKE YOU IN JESUS NAME. LEARN TO PLEAD THE BLOOD OF JESUS FOR YOUR NEEDS. STAND ON REV. 12:11---FOR THEY OVERCAME HIM BY THE BLOOD OF THE LAMB AND BY THE WORD OF THEIR TESTIMONY. KNOW SATAN IS A DEFEATED FOE AND REMIND HIM OF IT!! KNOW YOU HAVE AUTHORITY OVER HIM IN JESUS NAME. STAND ON LUKE 10:19. LEARN TO BIND SATAN AND HIS DEMONS BY THIS AUTHORITY USING MATT. 18:18---WHAT IS BOUND ON EARTH IS BOUND IN HEAVEN AND ALSO LEARN TO LOOSE GOD'S WILL AND SPIRIT ON EARTH USING MATT. 18:18---WHAT IS LOOSEN ON EARTH IS LOOSEN IN HEAVEN. LEARN TO PRAY GOD'S WILL USING MATT. 6:8. LEARN GOD'S WILL FOR YOU AND CLAIM IT---III JOHN 2. ASK FOR GOD'S BLESSING DAILY USE NUMBERS 6:24-26.---ROMANS 8:28-

--WE KNOW THAT GOD CAUSES ALL THINGS TO WORK TOGETHER FOR GOOD TO THOSE WHO LOVE GOD AND TO THOSE WHO ARE CALLED ACCORDING TO HIS PURPOSE. AND LAST BUT NOT LEAST----IN ALL THINGS GIVE THANKS!!!

A RIGHTEOUS MAN MAY HAVE MANY TROUBLES BUT THE LORD DELIVERS HIM FROM THEM ALL. FOR HE WILL COMMAND HIS ANGELS CONCERNING YOU TO GUARD YOU IN ALL YOUR WAYS. TO YOU, O LORD, I LIFT UP MY SOUL; IN YOU I TRUST, O MY GOD. LET NOT MY ENEMIES TRIUMPH OVER ME. A RIGHTEOUS MAN WILL HAVE NO FEAR OF BAD NEWS; HIS HEART IS STEADFAST, TRUSTING IN THE LORD. HIS HEART IS SECURE, HE WILL HAVE NO FEAR, IN THE END HE WILL LOOK IN TRIUMPH ON HIS FOES. "BECAUSE HE LOVES ME" SAYS THE LORD, "I WILL RESCUE HIM; I WILL PROTECT HIM FOR HE ACKNOWLEDGES MY NAME. HE WILL CALL UPON ME, AND I WILL ANSWER HIM; I WILL BE WITH HIM IN TROUBLE. I WILL DELIVER HIM AND HONOR HIM WITH LONG LIFE WILL I SATISFY HIM AND SHOW HIM MY SALVATION.

WHEN HARD TIMES COME

THANKS BE TO GOD WHO GIVETH THE VICTORY
THROUGH THE LORD JESUS CHRIST

We overcome by the blood of the Lamb and the word of our testimony.(Rev. 12:11) Though I walk in the midst of trouble, thou wilt revive me.(Ps. 138:7) But he knoweth the way that I take: when he hath tried me, I shall come forth as gold. (Job 23:10) I would like to share with everyone knowledge of the believer's authority, so you can grow and use your own authority, because the time will come when you will have to use your own authority if you want your prayers answered. All the authority that was given to Christ belongs to us through Him, and we may exercise it. In our battle against the enemy and his forces, we need to keep in mind

that we're above them and our job is to enforce His victory. His victory belongs to us, but we are to carry it out. If we don't do something, Jesus can't. This may come as a surprise to some. But we as believers are told to do something about the devil. The reason is because you have authority to do it. When Jesus arose from the dead, all power was given to him in heaven and in earth. Then he immediately delegated his authority on earth to the Church(us his children) and he can work only through us the body for he is the Head. The very first sign mentioned as following any believer, is that they shall cast out devils. That means that in Jesus Name we shall exercise authority over the devil because Jesus has delegated his authority over the devil to the Church(us his children). If you don't do anything about the devil and his forces, nothing will be done. Now you can understand why things happen as they have. We've, from lack of knowledge, permitted them to happen! That's a big responsibility, but never the less, warfare belongs to the body to perform. Ignorance is no accuse. We must learn and perform spiritual warfare. Our family, church, community, country, and world depends on us the body. Not knowing our authority---not knowing what we could do---we have done nothing, and we actually have permitted the devil to keep on doing whatever he wants to do. Wake Up! The devil has been walking on us too long. We need to put him on the run. GOD's plan for us is that we rule and reign in life over circumstances, poverty, disease, and everything else that would hinder us. We reign because we have authority. We reign by JESUS CHRIST. GOD didn't intend for the devil to dominate our families. When we understand what belongs to us, we will enjoy the victory Christ has for us. The devil will fight to keep us from getting there but through stubborn faith in Christ, the victory can be ours! Heaven will back us up on what we refuse and what we allow. We're waiting on GOD and He's waiting on us, and He won't do anything until we act. We have a part to play and we must cooperate with the Lord in faith. The Lord is hindered in His plan because His body has failed to exercise their authority. Put the Word first and the Spirit second and understand with your heart. We Christians, his body, must put on the whole armor of GOD and engage in spiritual warfare by doing the works of JESUS and taking our authority over the devil as we go about our daily lives. We are to interfere with Satan's kingdom by exercising our spiritual authority; he will attack you in an attempt to get you to back down from using that authority. You may as well get ready for these attacks, because they're coming. This spiritual position makes you an enemy to the devil. The believer must continually be arrayed with GOD's armor.(Ephesians 6:10-18) Any time you get into the Word of GOD, you enter into more intensive warfare with the enemy. Every piece of the Christians armor is related to the Word of GOD. Let's sharpen up our swords. As long as Satan can keep you in unbelief or hold you in the arena of reason, he'll whip you in every battle. But if you'll hold him in the arena of faith and the spirit, you will whip him every time. Let him know "I demand my rights!" You've got to learn what your rights are. Therefore, in our battle against the enemy and his forces, we need to keep in mind that we're above them and have authority over them. Our job is to enforce JESUS' victory. The believer is told to do something about the devil. The reason is because you have the authority to do it. We're not to pray about the devil and his deeds, we are to exercise our authority over all evil, the authority that belongs to us the Body. In Luke 10:19, we are given authority over all evil. In Matt. 28:18 JESUS delegated all power to the CHURCH(his body). GOD can only work through the Body in the Name of JESUS. In Mark 16:15-18, the first sign mentioned following a believer is they shall cast out demons. Col. 1:13 delivered us fro the authority of darkness, Satan and his kingdom, therefore we've got the right to speak to darkness and tell them what to do. James 4:7 tells us to resist the devil, and he will flee from you. John 4:4 tells greater is he in me than he that is in the world. Hosea 4:6 tells my people perish for lack of knowledge. Ephesians 1:21 says JESUS is name above all names. John 14:12 says greater works shall we do. John 14:13 tells we should ask in JESUS name. I Peter 5 describes Satan as a roaring lion seeking those he may devour. Those are the parts of the body lacking in the knowledge that he don't have the authority to do so. Satan's kingdom is like an army. They have ranks and assignments. Demons are evil personalities. They are spirit beings without a body. They must use humans to work through. They are enemies of GOD and man. Their objectives in humans beings are to tempt, deceive, accuse, condemn, pressure, defile, resist, oppose, control, steal, afflict, kill, and destroy. Demons enter through open doors. They have to be given an opportunity. The door for demons to enter may be opened by oneself through sins of omission and commission. Demons can also be attached to objects and animals. Spiritual house cleaning is a necessary part of warfare. There is not a person on the face of the earth who escapes his notice. He devises a plan to ruin and destroy each one of us. You and I are definite targets of Satan's wiles. Demon spirits can invade and indwell human bodies. Christians are not immune. The Christian should always consider indwelling demons as unnecessary and undesirable Trespassers. A trespasser is one who unlawfully and stealthily encroaches upon the territory of another. Trespassers can continue their unlawful practices until they are confronted and challenged on the basis of one's legal rights. No demon can remain when the Christian seriously desires him to go! But let's face it, some of us choose to keep demons attached to our secret sins. We don't want to turn those sins loose, but we must. All demons are liars and deceivers. Demons have no title to bodies redeemed by the blood of the Lord JESUS CHRIST. Demon spirits only defile. Demons are spiritual enemies and it is the responsibility of each Christian to deal with them directly in spiritual warfare. The battle is very personal and close. The enemy is a spiritual one. The weapons are spiritual. The Christian soldier has great authority. He is vested with the authority in the name of JESUS. The Christian Warrior has the promise of GOD's Word that he can have greater power than that of the enemy. It is imperative that we recognize Satan to be a defeated foe. We have every right to treat him as a trespasser. The more Christians enter into warfare, the more Satan will suffer losses. We wrestle against spiritual wickedness in High places. Most Christians have not become engaged in spiritual battle because they have never been taught the importance of it nor the way to go about it. GOD is raising up a mighty army today that is going forth with spiritual weapons. GOD's people are being set free from torments of demon spirits. Satan has a method---a settled plan---to conquer each one of us along with our families, church, community and nation. GOD has provided Armor for our protection and weapons for offensive warfare. This is the starting point for total spiritual warfare. The first objective in the warfare is to free oneself. We must learn how to get him out and keep him out. Talk out loud to the demons!! It is an effective and necessary tactic of spiritual warfare. Demons talk to our minds, it is the way they plant seeds of resentment and suspicion. Command them to leave you alone, in the name of JESUS. Do not stop at telling them once. Demons can be stubborn, so keep resisting until your mind is at peace. We must realize demons take advantage of sins and circumstances in life. In many homes today, even though husband, wife and children may profess Christ, there is strife, division, confusion, and chaos. It is time families learn how to drive the devil out of their homes and lives. WARFARE is not Prayer. It is in addition to prayer. GOD has given us power and authority over the devil. We must not expect GOD to get the devil off our backs. He has already defeated Satan and given us the ability and responsibility to take care of ourselves. Satan has a special interest in the church. These prince spirits over churches can be bound and their voices silenced. GOD has given the power to His body. It is up to them to do it. Satan has assigned a powerful demon ruler over every nation of the world, and in turn, over every city, community, church and person. Our problems are basically spiritual. GOD has given us spiritual weapons and resourced for victory. The body has the answer. It must take the offensive against the ranks of demonic powers while there is yet time. By vocalizing your position in Christ and your authority over these demon forces. The process of expelling demons is called deliverance. Many Christians today are finding real help through deliverance. Problems that could not be solved through known avenues of help are now being solved through deliverance. It makes us wonder why we have been so long in seeing these truths in GOD's Word. Some of the most common symptoms of indwelling demons are emotional problems, mental problems, speech problems, sex problems, addictions, physical infirmities, and religious error. When we obey we have fellowship with the Lord and we obtain His love, His joy and His peace. When we disobey, fellowship with GOD is broken and Satan has gained a way of entrance. When demon spirits are cast out they normally leave through the mouth or nose. Spirits are associated with breathing. The most common manifestation is coughing often with phlegm. Vomiting, drooling, spitting, or foaming is common. Infrequently small amounts of blood may appear. It is not unusual for this material to flow out of a person for an hour or longer. Other manifestations include crying, screaming, sighing, roaring, belching, and yawning. One must be honest with himself and with GOD if he expects to receive GOD's blessing of deliverance. Ask GOD to help you see yourself as He sees you and bring to light anything that is not of Him. We must recognize that one is dependent upon GOD and His provisions for deliverance. Repentance is a determined turning away from sin and Satan. Repentance requires open confession of all sin. It takes away the legal rights of demon spirits. Renunciation is the forsaking of evil. It means a clean break with Satan and all his works. Willingness to forgive is absolutely essential to deliverance. Ask GOD to deliver you and set you free in the name of JESUS. Prayer and warfare are two separate and distinct activities. Prayer is toward GOD and warfare is toward the enemy. Praise silences the enemy. Praise is not an attitude of the heart; it is the expression unto GOD of thankfulness, adoration and joy. Pray in the spirit and without ceasing. Take up your cross daily and follow JESUS. Break old habit patterns set up in league with evil spirits. Keep yourself under GOD's authority. Faith and trust in GOD is the greatest weapon against the devils lies. Walk in daily deliverance. Do not settle for anything less! Once delivered the house must be filled and kept filled with the fruits of the Spirit; love, joy, peace, longsuffering, gentleness, goodness, faith, meekness and temperance. We are not looking for ways to make demons easier to live with but how to get rid of them. Demons are spiritual enemies and it is the responsibility of each Christian to deal with them directly in spiritual warfare. We must throw away ineffective fleshly weapons and take up the mighty spiritual weapons. The believer must know both his own weaponry, how to employ it and the tactics of the enemy and how to defeat him. The power of the believer comes to him with the baptism in the Holy Spirit. We need both authority and power to deal with the enemy. Satan is stripped of his power and his kingdom. We have every right to treat him as a trespasser. We can be set free from the torments

of demon spirits. Intruders can be driven out and the doors closed behind them. Command them to come out In JESUS NAME. Absolutely renounce them, speaking in faith and they will respond. DO NOT LET THEM GO UNCHALLENGED ANOTHER DAY !!!

LOVE LETTERS FROM GOD

2 a.m. --- 5 a.m. MARCH 24, 2002 PALM SUNDAY

The mystery that has been kept hidden for ages and generations is now disclosed to the saints. And whatever you do in word or deed do it all in the name of the LORD JESUS giving thanks to GOD the FATHER through him. Devote yourselves to prayer, being watchful and thankful. For the LORD himself will come down from heaven with a loud command, with the voice of the archangel and with the trumpet call of GOD and the dead in Christ will rise first. Be joyful, always pray, continually give thanks in all circumstances. I want all men everywhere to lift up holy hands in prayer without anger or disputing.

Grace, mercy and peace from GOD the Father and from Jesus Christ, the Father's Son will be with us in truth and love.

I waited patiently for the LORD: Now I say "Here I am, I have come ---------- it is written, about me in the scroll. I desire to do your will, O my GOD; your law is within my heart. I proclaim righteousness in this great assembly; I do not hide your righteousness in heart; I speak of your faithfulness and salvation. I do not conceal your love and your truth from this great assembly. Many, O LORD my GOD, are the wonders you have done. Things you have planned for us no one can recount to you, were I to speak and tell of them, they would be too many to declare. The salvation of the righteous comes from the LORD; he is their stronghold in time of trouble. The LORD helps them; he delivers them. He delivers them from the wicked and saves them because they take refuge in Him. O LORD so not forsake me, be not far from me, O my GOD. I have waited for you, O LORD; you will answer, O LORD my GOD. You have wearied the Lord with your words by saying "All who do evil are good in the eyes of the Lord and he is pleased with them" or "Where is the GOD of justice?" See, I will send my messenger, who will prepare the way before me, the messenger of whom you desire has come, says the LORD ALMIGHTY. Now those who fear the Lord will talk with each other and the Lord will listen and hear. A scroll of remembrance was written in his presence concerning those who fear the Lord and honored His name. "They will be mine" says the Lord Almighty, in the day when I make up my treasured possession. I will spare them just as in compassion a man spares his son who serves him. And you will again see the distinction between the righteous and the wicked, between those who serve GOD and those who do not. Surely the day is coming. All the arrogant and every evildoer will be stubble, and that day that is coming will set them on fire, says the LORD ALMIGHTY. But for you who revere my name, the sun of righteousness will rise with healing in it's wings. And you will go out and leap like calves released from stall. Then you will trample down the wicked, they will be ashes under the soles of your feet on the day when I do these says the Lord Almighty. See I send you a prophet before that great day she will turn the hearts of the fathers to their children and the hearts of the children to their fathers. The chosen lady and the children walking in truth, whom I love in the truth. The truth whom which lives in us and will be with us forever, just as the Father commanded us. I am not writing you a new command but one we have had from the beginning. I ask that we love one another and this is the love that we walk in obedience to his commands. As you have heard from the beginning his command is that you walk in love. Many deceivers, who do not acknowledge Jesus Christ as coming in the flesh, have gone out into the world. Any such person is the deceiver and the antichrist. Watch out that you are not deceived. The time is near. Do not follow them. They will lay hands on you and persecute you all on account of my name. But make up your mind not to worry before hand how you will defend yourselves. For I will give you words and wisdom that none of your adversaries will be able to resist or contradict. All men will hate you because of me but not a hair of your head will perish. By standing firm you will gain life. When you see these things happening you know that the kingdom of GOD is near. For there is nothing hidden that will not be disclosed and nothing concealed that will not be known or brought out into the open. Therefore, consider how you listen. Whoever has will be given more; whoever does not have even what he thinks he has will be taken from him. For everyone who asks receives, he who seeks finds and to him who knocks the door will be opened. Good gifts to GOD's children will your Father in heaven give the Holy Spirit to those who ask him, not because of his own purpose and grace. This grace was given us in Christ Jesus before the beginning of time. Be strong in the grace that is in Christ Jesus. Endure hardships like a good soldier of Christ Jesus. For GOD did not give us a spirit of timidity, but a spirit of power, of love and of self-discipline. Guard the good deposit that was entrusted to you - guard it with the help of the Holy Spirit. Remember JESUS CHRIST that is risen from the dead, with eternal glory. If we died with him; we will also live with him. If we endure we will also reign with him. If we disown him he will also disown us. If we are faithless, he will remain faithful for he cannot disown himself.

In the presence of GOD and of CHRIST JESUS, who will judge the living and the dead and in view of his appearing and his kingdom; I give you charge. Preach the word, be prepared in season and out of season, correct, rebuke and encourage--with great patience and careful instruction. For the time had come when men will not put up with sound doctrine. Instead, to suit their own desires they have gathered around them a great number of teachers to say what their itching ears want to hear. They have turned away from the truth and turned aside to myths. These people honor me with their lips but their hearts are far from me. They worship me in vain, their teachings are but rules taught by men. For from within, out of men's hearts, come evil thoughts, sexual immorality, theft, murder, adultery, greed, malice, deceit, lewdness, envy, slander, arrogance and folly. Listen to me, everyone and understand this. You have a fine way of setting aside the commands of GOD in order to observe your own traditions. Thus you nullify the word of GOD by your traditions that you have handed down. You have let go of the commands of GOD and are holding on to the traditions of men. Why do you break the commands of GOD for the sake of your traditions? Listen and understand. Blessed are your eyes because they see and your ears because they hear. A wicked and adulterous generation asks for a miraculous sign. But none will be given it except the sign of Jonah. The Queen of the South will rise at the judgment with the men of this generation and condemn them for she came from the ends of the earth to listen to Solomon's wisdom and now one greater than Solomon is here. Let it be so now worship the Lord your GOD and serve him only. Come follow me and I will make you fishers of men. Repent for the kingdom of heaven is near. You are the salt of the earth. You are the light of the world. Let your light shine before men that they may see your good deeds and praise your Father in heaven. Store up for yourselves treasures in heaven. For where your treasure is there your heart will be also. Small is the gate and narrow the road that leads to life. Therefore, everyone who hears these words of mine and put them into practice is like a wise man that built his house on the rock. The harvest is plentiful but the workers are few. As you go preach this message: The kingdom of heaven is near. Heal the sick. Freely you have received freely give. Do not be afraid. What is whispered in your ear proclaim from the roofs. Whoever acknowledges me before men I will also acknowledge him before my Father in heaven. Whoever finds his life will lose it and whoever loses his life for my sake will find it. This is the one about whom it is written: I will send my messenger who will prepare your way before you. I praise you Father, Lord of heaven and earth because you have hidden these things from the wise and learned and revealed them to little children. He who is not with me is against me. Men will give account for every careless word they speak. For by your words you will be acquitted and by your words you will be condemned. The righteous will shine like the sun in the kingdom of their Father. He who has ears let him hear. For the Son of Man is going to come in His Father's glory with His angels and then He will reward each person according to what he has done. I tell you the truth some who are standing here will not taste death before they see the Son of Man coming in His kingdom. Get up! Don't be afraid! Love the Lord your GOD with all your heart and all your soul and all your mind. All these are the beginning of birth pains. And this gospel of the kingdom will be preached in the whole world as a testimony to all nations and then the end will come. Therefore keep watch because no one knows about the day or hour not even the angels in heaven nor the Son but only the Father. Therefore, go and make disciples of all nations; baptizing them in the name of the Father and of the Son and of the Holy Spirit. Teaching them to obey everything I have commanded you. And surely I am with you always, to the very end of the age. The time has come, the kingdom of GOD is near. Repent and believe the good news!! Don't be afraid just believe. I raised you up for this very purpose that I might display my power in you and that my name might be proclaimed in all the earth. For the Lord will carry out his sentence on earth with speed and finality. If you confess with your mouth Jesus is Lord and believe in your heart that GOD raised him from the dead you will be saved. We have different gifts according to the grace given us. So let us put aside the deeds of darkness and put on the armor of light. Therefore glorify Christ Jesus in your service to GOD. May the GOD of hope fill you with all joy and peace, as you trust in him; so that you may overflow with hope by the power of the Holy Spirit. Not in words taught us by human wisdom but in words taught by the spirit expressing spiritual truths in spiritual words. For the wisdom of this world is foolishness in GOD's sight. For this world in it's present form is passing away. The earth is the Lord's and everything in it. No one can say Jesus is Lord except by the Holy Spirit. Not according to worldly wisdom but according to GOD's grace; in order that Satan might not outwit us. So from now on we regard no one from a worldly point of view. For though we live in this world, we do not wage war as the world does. We demolish arguments and every pretension that sets itself up against the knowledge of GOD. We take captive every thought to make it obedient to Christ. If you belong to Christ then you are Abraham's seed and heirs to the promise. It is for freedom that Christ has set us free. Stand firm. Anyone who receives instruction in the word must share all good things. We are to prepare GOD's people for works of service so that the body of Christ may be built up, until we all reach unity in the faith and in the knowledge of the Son of GOD and become mature attaining to the whole measure of the fullness of Christ. For it is GOD who works in you to will and to act according to his good purpose. Let us hold unswervingly to the hope we profess for he who promised is faithful. Prepare your minds for action. The end of all things is near. Therefore be clear-minded and self-controlled so that you can pray. Be alert, your enemy the devil prowls around like a roaring lion looking for someone to devour. The reason the world does not know us is that it did not know him. The world hates you. GOD is love. Keep yourselves in GOD's love as you wait for the mercy of our Lord Jesus Christ to bring you to eternal life. Grace and Peace be with you always, Your Sister in Christ: Claudia ii tim 4 21.

MARCH 25, 2006 1:30 a.m.

I CHARGE YOU BEFORE THE LORD TO HAVE THIS LETTER READ TO ALL THE BROTHERS OF THE LORD CHRIST JESUS May GOD himself, the GOD of peace, sanctify you through and through. May your whole spirit, soul, and body be kept blameless at the coming of our Lord Jesus Christ. The one who calls you is faithful and he will do it. And we who are in Him who is true- even in His Son Jesus Christ. He is the true GOD and eternal life. To Him be glory forever and ever. The Lord be with your spirit. Grace and Peace be with you always. Thank GOD, because your faith is growing more, more. And the love for one another is increasing. You are enduring with perseverance and faith in all persecutions and trails. As a result you will be counted worthy of the Kingdom of GOD, for which you are suffering with this in mind, constantly pray that GOD will count you worthy of His calling and that by His power He may fulfill every good purpose of yours and every act prompted by your faith. May the Lord Jesus Christ be glorified in you. He will pay back trouble to those who trouble you and give relief to you who are troubled. May the Lord of peace Himself give you peace at all times

and in everyway. From the beginning, GOD chose you to be saved through the sanctifying work of the spirit and through belief in the Truth. He called you through the gospel that you might share in the glory of our Lord Jesus Christ. Now stand firm and hold to the teachings, passed on to you by word of mouth or written. May our Lord Jesus Christ encourage your hearts and strengthen you in every good deed and work. Pray that the message of the Lord may spread rapidly and be honored. Pray that we may be delivered from wicked and evil men for not everyone has faith. But the Lord is faithful and he will strengthen and protect you from the evil one. May the Lord direct your hearts into GOD's love and Christ's perseverance. Now, concerning the coming of our Lord Jesus Christ and our being gathered to Him we ask you not to become easily unsettled or alarmed. Don't let anyone deceive you in any way for that day will not come until the rebellion occurs and the man of lawlessness is revealed, the man doomed to destruction. He will oppose and will exalt himself over everything that is called GOD or is worshipped, so that he sets himself up in GOD's temple, proclaiming himself to be GOD. And now you know what is holding him back so that he may be revealed at the proper time. For the secret power of lawlessness is already at work; but the one who now holds it back and will continue to do so till he is taken out of the way. And then the lawless one will be revealed. This will happen when the Lord Jesus is revealed from heaven in blazing fire with His powerful angels. He will punish those who do not know GOD and do not obey the gospel of our Lord Jesus Christ. They will be punished with everlasting destruction and shut out from the presence of the Lord and from the majesty of His power and then the lawless one will be revealed whom the Lord Jesus will overthrow with the breath of His mouth and destroy by the splendor of His coming. They will perish because they refuse to love the truth and so be saved. All will be condemned who have not believed the truth but delight in wickedness. If anyone does not obey our instruction in this letter, take special note of him. Do not associate with him, in order that he may feel, ashamed. Yet do not regard him as an enemy, but warn him as a brother. The grace of our Lord Jesus Christ be with you all.

APRIL 6, 2008

O, my children, do not let our enemy, the devil, lead you into captivity of sin and disobedience; it leads only to destruction. Do not walk in the customs of the world. Do not do secretly against the Lord your GOD things not right. Doing these wicked things provokes the Lord to anger. Stop serving your modern day idols, the things you put before the Lord thy GOD. Turn from your evil ways and keep My commandments and My statues. Yet you will not hear and harden your hearts. You do not believe or trust in, rely on, and remain steadfast to the Lord your GOD. You despise and reject His statutes and His covenant. You do not heed His warnings. Your following vanity and your prayers will be empty and futile. You are going after the heathens (those that sin against the Lord) of whom the Lord has charged you not to do as they do. Therefore the Lord is very angry with America. He will remove you out of His sight. Therefore, the Lord will send lions among you. America does not know the manner in which the GOD of the land requires their worship. We must teach the people the law of the GOD of the land. Teach them how they should fear and revere the Lord. They fear

the Lord yet serve their own gods. You shall not fear other gods or bow yourself to them or serve them. But you shall reverently fear, bow yourself to and serve the Lord thy GOD. These shall you do forevermore. Then He will deliver you out of the hands of all your enemies. Do not do as the world and vainly fear the Lord while serving graven images. Get rid of the things that keep you from walking in obedience to GOD. What keeps you from obeying GOD? What seems very important to you? Ask GOD to help you do what is right in His eyes and know He will honor your obedience. Because your raging against the Lord, and your arrogance and careless ease have come to His ears, and you will not listen you are seduced to do more evil than the nations whom the Lord has destroyed. Because they have forsaken Me, provoking Me to anger with all the work of their hands, therefore My Wrath will be kindled against this place and it will not be quenched.

MATTHEW 4:19

"Come, follow me," Jesus said,
"and I will make you fishers of men."

IN REMEMBERANCE
OF OUR
FISHERS OF MEN

Devin Paul Jones
February 19, 2001 -- May 7, 2005

AND

Darin Edward Scott
October 8, 1990 -- October 19, 2007